Selenium 2 Testing Tools Beginner's Guide

Learn to use Selenium testing tools from scratch

David Burns

BIRMINGHAM - MUMBAI

Selenium 2 Testing Tools Beginner's Guide

First published: November 2010

Second published: October 2012

Production Reference: 1091012

Published by Packt Publishing Ltd.
Livery Place
35 Livery Street
Birmingham B3 2PB, UK.

ISBN 978-1-84951-830-7

www.packtpub.com

Cover Image by John M. Quick (john.m.quick@gmail.com)

Credits

Author

David Burns

Reviewers

Tarun Kumar Bhadauria

Dave Hunt

Acquisition Editor

Usha Iyer

Lead Technical Editor

Pramila Balan

Technical Editors

Joyslita D'Souza

Rohit Rajgor

Project Coordinator

Yashodhan Dere

Proofreader

Steve Maguire

Indexers

Monica Ajmera Mehta

Rekha Nair

Tejal R. Soni

Graphics

Aditi Gajjar

Production Coordinators

Melwyn D'sa

Arvindkumar Gupta

Cover Work

Melwyn D'sa

Arvindkumar Gupta

About the Author

David Burns is a Senior Developer in Test having worked with Selenium for quite a few years. He is a Selenium Core Committer and so he knows and understands what users and developers want from the framework.

> I would like to thank everyone in the Selenium community for making this product the great tool it is, and giving me an opportunity to write the Second Edition of this book!

About the Reviewers

Tarun Kumar Bhadauria has been associated with software testing industry from more than seven years. His primary interest is towards manual testing and he equally enjoys using Selenium for automated testing of web applications. He has been using Selenium from the days of Selenium Remote Control. He has co-authored the official Selenium doc available at SeleniumHQ. He is working as a Test Engineer at Pontiflex.

Dave Hunt lives in Kent, UK, with his wife and young son. He has always had a passion for turning mundane tasks into one-click solutions, and when he discovered Selenium back in 2005, his career in software testing and automation development was sealed. He works from home for Mozilla, where he assists teams to create automated tests for their projects—ranging from Mozilla's web properties to the Firefox web browser and the Thunderbird e-mail client.

www.PacktPub.com

Support files, eBooks, discount offers and more

You might want to visit www.PacktPub.com for support files and downloads related to your book.

Did you know that Packt offers eBook versions of every book published, with PDF and ePub files available? You can upgrade to the eBook version at www.PacktPub.com and as a print book customer, you are entitled to a discount on the eBook copy. Get in touch with us at service@packtpub.com for more details.

At www.PacktPub.com, you can also read a collection of free technical articles, sign up for a range of free newsletters and receive exclusive discounts and offers on Packt books and eBooks.

http://PacktLib.PacktPub.com

Do you need instant solutions to your IT questions? PacktLib is Packt's online digital book library. Here, you can access, read and search across Packt's entire library of books.

Why Subscribe?

◆ Fully searchable across every book published by Packt
◆ Copy and paste, print and bookmark content
◆ On demand and accessible via web browser

Free Access for Packt account holders

If you have an account with Packt at www.PacktPub.com, you can use this to access PacktLib today and view nine entirely free books. Simply use your login credentials for immediate access.

To my loving wife and my amazing boy for giving me the support and drive to finish this book! I love you both!

Table of Contents

Preface

Selenium WebDriver is the most used tool for browser automation. This book shows developers and testers how to create automated tests using a browser. You will learn how to be able to use Selenium IDE for quick throwaway tests. Or if you want to create tests to last, learn to use Selenium WebDriver.

You will learn to use Selenium WebDriver with both desktop browsers and mobile browsers, and learn good design patterns to make sure your tests will be extremely maintainable.

What this book covers

Chapter 1, *Getting Started with Selenium IDE*, explains how to install Selenium IDE and record our first tests. We will see what is needed to work against AJAX applications.

Chapter 2, *Locators*, shows how we can find elements on the page to be used in our tests. We will use XPath, CSS, Link Text, and ID to find elements on the page so that we can interact with them.

Chapter 3, *Overview of Selenium WebDriver*, discusses all the history and architectural designs for Selenium WebDriver. You will also go through the necessary items for setting up a development environment.

Chapter 4, *Design Patterns*, introduces the different design patterns that can be used with Selenium WebDriver. The design patterns will show you how to make your tests more maintainable and allow more people to work on your code.

Chapter 5, *Finding Elements*, explains all the different techniques to find elements with Selenium WebDriver. This chapter builds on the locators that we learnt in *Chapter 2*, *Locators*.

Chapter 6, *Working with WebDriver*, introduces all the different aspects of getting different browsers that Selenium WebDriver supports on desktop operating systems.

Chapter 7, Mobile Devices, explains how Selenium WebDriver works on mobile devices to test mobile websites or sites built with responsive web design.

Chapter 8, Getting Started with Selenium Grid, shows us how we can set up our Selenium Grid. We will also take a look at running tests in parallel to try bringing down the time it takes to run tests.

Chapter 9, Advanced User Interactions, explains how to build chains of actions together to help when you need to drag-and-drop or have key combinations working. We will also look at how we can press a mouse button and hold it down while we move the mouse.

Chapter 10, Working with HTML5, explains working with some of the HTML5 technologies that are becoming available to browsers. The Selenium WebDriver APIs are very similar to the JavaScript APIs in the browser to try make use of them easier.

Chapter 11, Advanced Topics, explains how to capture network traffic between the browser and the web server. We finish off by capturing screenshots.

Appendix A, Migrating from Remote Control to WebDriver, introduces how the interaction with the browser has changed and how we can convert our Selenium 1 tests to Selenium 2 to take advantage of the changes in Selenium WebDriver.

What you need for this book

- Mozilla Firefox
- Google Chrome
- Internet Explorer
- Opera
- Intellij IDEA
- Firebug
- Firefinder
- Selenium IDE
- Selenium Grid
- Ubuntu Linux

Who this book is for

If you are a Software Quality Assurance professional, Software Project Manager, or a Software Developer interested in automated testing using Selenium, this book is for you. Web-based application developers will also benefit from this book.

Conventions

In this book, you will find several headings appearing frequently.

To give clear instructions of how to complete a procedure or task, we use:

Time for action – heading

1. Action 1
2. Action 2
3. Action 3

Instructions often need some extra explanation so that they make sense, so they are followed with:

What just happened?

This heading explains the working of tasks or instructions that you have just completed.

You will also find some other learning aids in the book, including:

Pop quiz – heading

These are short multiple choice questions intended to help you test your own understanding.

Have a go hero – heading

These set practical challenges and give you ideas for experimenting with what you have learned.

You will also find a number of styles of text that distinguish between different kinds of information. Here are some examples of these styles, and an explanation of their meaning.

Code words in text are shown as follows: "We do this by running `java-jar selenium-server.jar` from a command prompt or from a terminal depending on your operating system."

A block of code is set as follows:

```
@Before

public void setUp(){
  selenium = new FirefoxDriver();
}
```

Any command-line input or output is written as follows:

```
-jar selenium-server-standalone.jar
```

New terms and **important words** are shown in bold. Words that you see on the screen, in menus or dialog boxes for example, appear in the text like this: "Select **Selenium Grid** from the drop-down box."

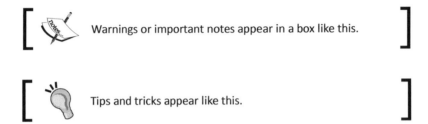

> Warnings or important notes appear in a box like this.

> Tips and tricks appear like this.

Reader feedback

Feedback from our readers is always welcome. Let us know what you think about this book—what you liked or may have disliked. Reader feedback is important for us to develop titles that you really get the most out of.

To send us general feedback, simply send an e-mail to feedback@packtpub.com, and mention the book title through the subject of your message.

If there is a topic that you have expertise in and you are interested in either writing or contributing to a book, see our author guide on www.packtpub.com/authors.

Customer support

Now that you are the proud owner of a Packt book, we have a number of things to help you to get the most from your purchase.

Errata

Although we have taken every care to ensure the accuracy of our content, mistakes do happen. If you find a mistake in one of our books—maybe a mistake in the text or the code—we would be grateful if you would report this to us. By doing so, you can save other readers from frustration and help us improve subsequent versions of this book. If you find any errata, please report them by visiting http://www.packtpub.com/support, selecting your book, clicking on the **errata submission form** link, and entering the details of your errata. Once your errata are verified, your submission will be accepted and the errata will be uploaded to our website, or added to any list of existing errata, under the Errata section of that title.

Piracy

Piracy of copyright material on the Internet is an ongoing problem across all media. At Packt, we take the protection of our copyright and licenses very seriously. If you come across any illegal copies of our works, in any form, on the Internet, please provide us with the location address or website name immediately so that we can pursue a remedy.

Please contact us at copyright@packtpub.com with a link to the suspected pirated material.

We appreciate your help in protecting our authors, and our ability to bring you valuable content.

Questions

You can contact us at questions@packtpub.com if you are having a problem with any aspect of the book, and we will do our best to address it.

1

Getting Started with Selenium IDE

Test automation is growing in popularity over the years because teams do not have the time or money to invest in large test teams to make sure that applications work as they are expected. Developers also want to make sure that the code they have created works as they expect it to.

Jason Huggins saw this issue too and wanted to make sure that a system he was working on would work on multiple operating systems and browsers. He created Selenium.

Selenium is one of the most well known testing frameworks in the world that is in use. It is an open source project that allows testers and developers alike to develop functional tests to drive the browser. It can be used to record workflows so that developers can prevent future regressions of code. Selenium can work on any browser that supports JavaScript, since Selenium has been built using JavaScript.

In this chapter we shall cover:

- What is Selenium IDE
- Recording our first test
- Updating tests to work with AJAX sites
- Using variables in our tests
- Debugging tests
- Saving tests to be used later
- Creating and saving test suites

So let's get on with it...

Important preliminary points

Before we start working through this chapter we need to make sure that Mozilla Firefox is installed on your machine. If you do not have Mozilla Firefox installed you will need to download it from `http://www.getfirefox.com/`.

What is Selenium IDE

Selenium IDE is a Firefox Add-on developed originally by Shinya Kasatani as a way to use the original Selenium Core code without having to copy Selenium Core onto the server. Selenium Core is the key JavaScript modules that allow Selenium to drive the browser. It has been developed using JavaScript so that it can interact with **DOM (Document Object Model)** using native JavaScript calls.

Selenium IDE was developed to allow testers and developers to record their actions as they follow the workflow that they need to test.

Time for action – installing Selenium IDE

Now that we understand what Selenium IDE is, it is a good time to install it. At the end of these steps, you will have successfully installed Selenium IDE on to your computer:

1. Go to `http://seleniumhq.org/download/`.

2. Click on the download link for Selenium IDE. You may see a message appear saying **Firefox prevented this site (seleniumhq.org) from asking you to install software on your computer**. If you do, click the **Allow** button.

3. A Firefox prompt will appear, as shown in the following screenshot:

4. You will then be asked if you would like to install Selenium IDE and the exporter add-ons. These have been made pluggable to the IDE by the work that Adam Goucher did. You will see a screen like the following appear:

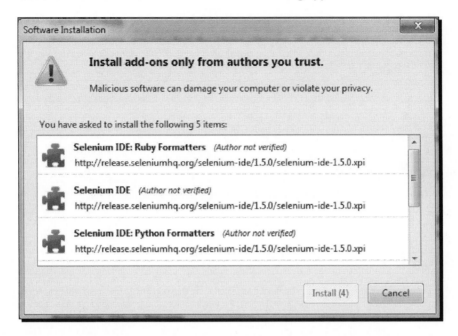

5. Once the countdown has finished on the **Install** button, it will become active; click it. This will now install Selenium IDE and formatters as Firefox Add-ons.

6. Once the install process is complete it will ask you to restart Firefox. Click the **Restart Now** button. Firefox will close and then re-open. If you have anything open in another browser it might be worth saving your work, as Firefox will try to go back to its original state but this cannot be guaranteed.

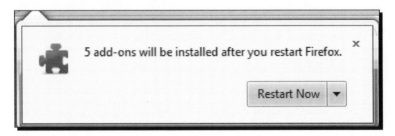

7. Once the installation is complete, the Add-ons window will show the Selenium IDE and its current version:

What just happened?

You have successfully installed Selenium IDE and we can start thinking about writing our first test.

Selenium IDE

Selenium IDE has been installed, so let's take some time to familiarize ourselves with Selenium IDE. This will give us the foundation that we can use in later chapters.

Open up Selenium IDE by going through the tools menu in Mozilla Firefox. The steps are **Tools | Selenium IDE**. A window will appear. If the menu bar is not available, which is now the default in Firefox, you can launch Selenium IDE via **Firefox | Web Developer | Selenium IDE**.

Starting from the top, I will explain what each of the items are:

- Base URL: This is the URL that the test will start at. All open commands will be relative to the Base URL unless a full path is inserted in the open command.
- Speed Slider: This is the slider under the **Fast** and **Slow** labels on the screen.
- ▶▤ Run all the tests in the IDE.
- ▶▪ Run a single test in the IDE.
- ▐▐ Pause a test that is currently running.
- ▨ Step through the test once it has paused.
- ⬤ This is the record button. This will be engaged when the test is recording.
- The **Command** selectbox has a list of all the commands that are needed to create a test. You can type into it to use the auto complete functionality or use it as a dropdown.
- The **Target** textbox allows you to input the location of the element that you want to work against.
- The **Find** button, once the target box is populated, can be clicked to highlight the element on the page.
- The **Value** textbox is where you place the value that needs to change. For example, if you want your test to type in an input box on the web page, you would put what you want it to type in the value box.
- The **Test** table will keep track of all your commands, targets, and values. It has been structured this way because the original version of Selenium was styled on FIT tests. FIT was created by Ward Cunningham and means Framework for Integrated Testing. The tests were originally designed to be run from HTML files and the IDE keeps this idea for its tests.
- If you click the **Source** tab you will be able to see the HTML that will store the test. Each of the rows will look like:

```
<tr>
  <td>open</td>
  <td>/chapter1</td>
  <td></td>
</tr>
```

◆ The area below the **Value** textbox will show the Selenium log while the tests are running. If an item fails, then it will have an `[error]` entry.
This area will also show help on Selenium Commands when you are working in the Command selectbox. This can be extremely useful when typing commands into Selenium IDE instead of using the record feature.

◆ The **Log** tab will show a log of what is happening during the test. The **Reference** tab gives you documentation on the command that you have highlighted.

Important note: Rules for automation

Now that we have installed Selenium IDE and understood what it is, we can think about working through our first tests. There are a few things that we need to consider when creating your first test. These rules apply to any form of test automation but need to be adhered to especially when creating tests against a User Interface.

◆ Tests should always have a known starting point. In the context of Selenium, this could mean opening a certain page to start a workflow.

◆ Tests should not have to rely on any other tests to run. If a test is going to add something, do not have a separate test to delete it. This is to ensure that if something goes wrong in one test, it will not mean you have a lot of unnecessary failures to check.

◆ Tests should only test one thing at a time.

◆ Tests should clean up after themselves.

These rules, like most rules, can be broken. However, breaking them can mean that you may run into issues later on, and when you have hundreds, or even thousands of tests, these small issues can mean that large parts of a test suite are failing.

With these rules in mind let us create our first Selenium IDE test.

Time for action – recording your first test with Selenium IDE

We are going to record our first test using Selenium IDE. To start recording the tests we will need to start Mozilla Firefox. Once it has been loaded, you will need to start Selenium IDE. You will find it under the **Tools** dropdown menu in Mozilla Firefox or in the Web Developer dropdown menu. Once loaded it will look like the next screenshot. Note that the record button is engaged when you first load the IDE.

To start recording your tests let us do the following:

1. When in record mode, navigate to `http://book.theautomatedtester.co.uk/` `chapter1`.

↖ doesn't work.

Click on url then chapter 1 link.

2. On the Web Application do the following:

1. Click on the radio button.

2. Select another value from the drop-down box, for example, **Selenium RC**.

3. Click on the **Home Page** link.

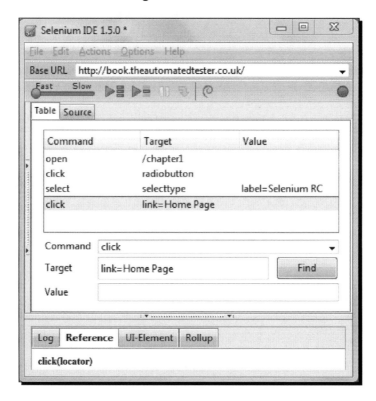

3. Your test has now been recorded and should look like the previous screenshot. Click the play button that looks like this: ▶=

4. Once your test has completed it will look like this:

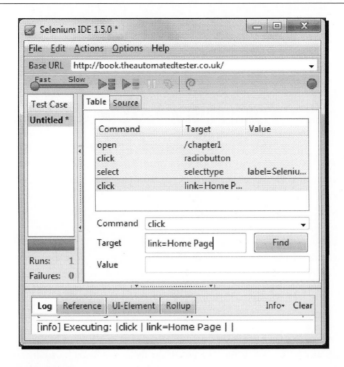

What just happened?

We have successfully recorded our first test and played it back. As we can see Selenium IDE has tried to apply the first rule of test automation by specifying the open command. It has set the starting point of the test, in this case /chapter1, and then it began stepping through the workflow that we want to record.

Once the actions have all been completed you will see that all of the actions have a green background. This shows that they have completed successfully. On the left you will see that it has completed one successful test, or run, within Selenium IDE. If you were to write a test that failed, the **Failure** label would have a 1 next to it.

Pop quiz – Selenium IDE

1. What is the main language that drives Selenium IDE?

   a. Ruby

   b. Python

   c. JavaScript

2. Selenium IDE works on Internet Explorer:
   a. True
   b. False

Updating a test to assert items are on the page

In the last few steps we were able to record a workflow that we would expect the user to perform. It will test that the relevant bit of functionality is there, like buttons and links to work against. Unfortunately we are not checking that the other items on the page are there or if they are visible when they should be hidden. We are going to work against the same page as before but we shall make sure that different items are on the page.

There are two mechanisms for validating elements available on the application under test. The first is **assert**; this allows the test to check if the element is on the page. If it is not available then the test will stop on the step that failed. The second is **verify**; this also allows the test to check the element is on the page, but if it isn't then the test will carry on executing.

To add the assert or verify commands to the tests we need to use the context menu that Selenium IDE adds to Firefox. All that one needs to do is right-click on the element if on Windows or Linux. If you have a Mac, then you will need to do the two finger click to show the context menu.

When the context menu appears, it will look roughly like the following screenshot with the normal Firefox functions above it:

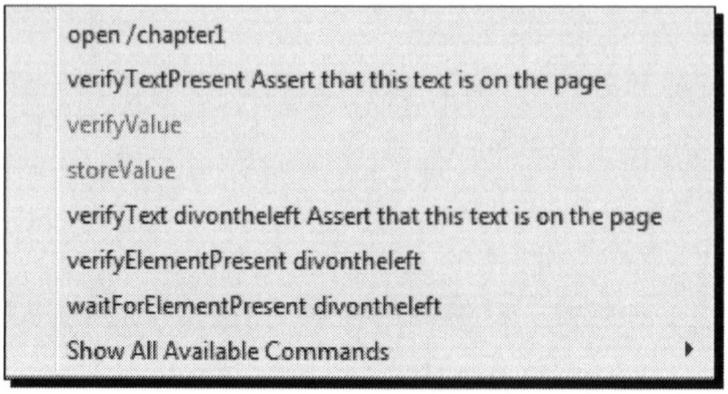

open /chapter1
verifyTextPresent Assert that this text is on the page
verifyValue
storeValue
verifyText divontheleft Assert that this text is on the page
verifyElementPresent divontheleft
waitForElementPresent divontheleft
Show All Available Commands ▸

[handwritten notes in left margin: Assert = stop test. Verify will allow test to continue]

Time for action – updating a test to verify items on the page

In this section we are going to be recording a test and then we are going to update it to have some verify commands:

1. Open the IDE so that we can start recording.

2. Navigate to `http://book.theautomatedtester.co.uk/chapter1`.

3. Select **Selenium Grid** from the drop-down box.

4. Change the **Select** to **Selenium Grid**.

5. Verify that Assert that this text is on the page text is mentioned on the right-hand side of the drop-down box, by right-clicking on the text and selecting Verify TextPresent **Assert that this text is on the page**. You can see the command in the previous screenshot.

6. Verify that the button is on the page. You will need to add a new command for `verifyElementPresent` with the target `verifybutton` in Selenium IDE.

7. Now that you have completed the previous steps, your Selenium IDE should look like the following screenshot:

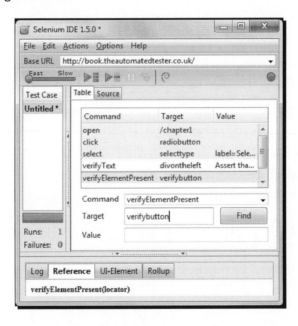

If you now run the test you will see it has verified that what you are expecting to see on the page has appeared. Notice that the verify commands have a darker green color. This is to show that they are more important to the test than moving through the steps. The test has now checked that the text we required is on the page and that the button was there too.

What would happen if the verify command did not find what it was expecting? The IDE would have thrown an Error stating what was expected was not there, but it carried on with the rest of the test. We can see an example of this in the following screenshot:

(handwritten margin note) Verify carries on and throws an error.

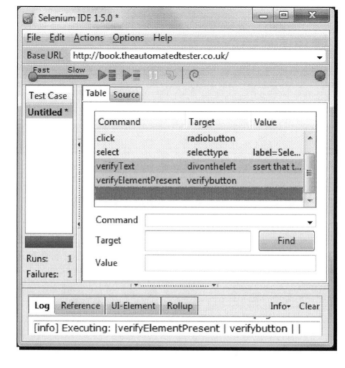

(handwritten margin note) Assert does NOT carry on

The test would not have carried on if it was using assert as the mechanism for validating that the elements and text were loaded with the page.

What just happened?

We have just seen that we can add Asserts or Verification to the page. Selenium IDE does not do this when recording, so it will always be a manual step. We saw that if we use the assert command it will cause the test to stop if it fails while the verify command allows the test to carry on after a failure. Each of these has their merits.

Have a go hero – recreating the test by using the assert methods

Some of the verify and assert methods are:

◆ verifyElementPresent
◆ assertElementPresent
◆ verifyElementNotPresent
◆ assertElementNotPresent
◆ verifyText
◆ assertText
◆ verifyAttribute ?   *Attribute = a piece of info that determines*
◆ assertAttribute ?   *the properties of a field/tag /or a*
◆ verifyChecked ?   *string of characters in a display*
◆ assertChecked ?
◆ verifyAlert ?
◆ assertAlert ?
◆ verifyTitle
◆ assertTitle

Pop quiz – verifying and asserting

1. Selenium verifies items on the page when it is recording steps:

    a. True
    b. False

2. What is the difference between verify and assert?   *Verify continues with test*
    Assert stops test & throws up
    error
    message

3. If you wanted to validate that a button has appeared on a page, which two commands would be the best to use?

    a. verifyTextPresent/assertTextPresent
    b. verifyElementPresent/assertElementPresent
    c. verifyAlertPresent/assertAlertPresent
    d. verifyAlert/assertAlert

Comments

Before we carry on further with Selenium, it would be a good time to mention how to create comments in your tests. As all good software developers know, having readable code and having comments can make maintenance in the future much easier. Unlike in software development it is extremely hard, almost impossible, to write self-documenting code. To combat this, it is good practice to make sure that your tests have comments that future software testers can use.

Time for action – adding Selenium IDE comments

To add comments to your tests do the following steps:

1. In the test that was created earlier, right-click on a step. For example, the verify step.

2. The Selenium IDE context menu will be visible as shown in the following screenshot:

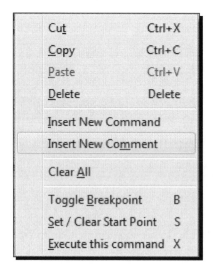

3. Click on **Insert New Comment**. A space will appear between the Selenium commands.

4. Click on the **Command** textbox and enter in a comment so that you can use it for future maintenance. It will look like the following screenshot:

What just happened?

We have just had a look at how to create comments. Comments will always appear as purple text in the IDE. This, like in most IDEs, is to help you spot comments quicker when looking through your test cases. Now that we know how to keep our tests maintainable with comments, let's carry on working with Selenium IDE to record/tweak/replay our scripts.

Multiplying windows

Web applications unfortunately do not live in one window of your browser. An example of this could be a site that shows reports. Most reports would have their own window so that people can easily move between them.

Unfortunately in testing terms this can be quite difficult to do, but in this section we will have a look at creating a test that can move between windows.

Time for action – working with multiple windows

Working with multiple browser windows can be one of the most difficult things to do within a Selenium Test. This is down to the fact that the browser needs to allow Selenium to programmatically know how many child browser processes have been spawned.

In the following examples we shall see the tests click on an element on the page which will cause a new window to appear. If you have a pop-up blocker running, it may be a good idea to disable it for this site while you work through these examples.

1. Open up Selenium IDE and go to the **Chapter 1** page on the site.

2. Click on one of the elements on the page that has the text **Click this link to launch another window**. This will cause a small window to appear.

3. Verify the text in the popup by right-clicking and selecting **VerifyText id=popup text within the popup window**.

4. Once the window has loaded, click on the **Close the Window** text inside it.

5. Add a verify command for an element on the page. Your test should now look like the following screenshot:

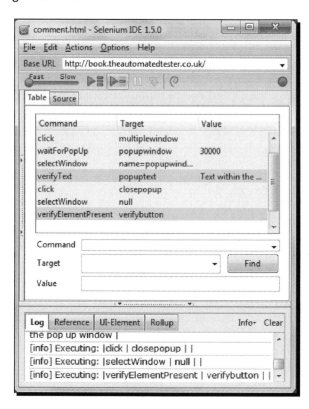

Sometimes Selenium IDE will add a `clickAndWait` instead of a click command. This is because it notices that the page has to unload. If this happens just change the `clickAndWait` to a click so that it does not cause a timeout in the test.

What just happened?

In the test script we can see that it has clicked on the item to load the new window and then has inserted a `waitForPopUp`. This is so that your test knows that it has to wait for a web server to handle the request and the browser to render the page. Any commands that require a page to load from a web server will have a `waitFor` command.

The next command is the `selectWindow` command. This command tells Selenium IDE that it will need to switch context to the window, called `popupwindow`, and will execute all the commands that follow in that window unless told otherwise by a later command.

Once the test has finished with the popup window, it will need to return to the parent window from where it started. To do this we need to specify `null` as the window. This will force the `selectWindow` to move the context of the test back to its parent window.

Time for action – complex working with multiple windows

In the next example we are going to open up two pop-up windows and move between them and the parent window as it completes its steps.

1. Start Selenium IDE and go to **Chapter 1** on the website.

2. Click on the **Click this link to launch another window** link. This will launch a pop-up window.

3. Assert the text on the page. We do this by right-clicking and selecting **assertText**.

4. Go back to the parent window and click on the link to launch the second pop-up window.

5. Verify the text on the page.

6. Move to the first pop-up window and close it using the close link. As before, be aware of `clickAndWait` instead of click.

7. Move to the second pop-up window and close it using the close link.

8. Move back to the parent window and verify an element on that page.

9. Run your test and watch how it moves between the windows. When complete it should look like the following screenshot:

What just happened?

We just had a look at creating a test that can move between multiple windows. We saw how we can move between the child windows and its parent window as though we were a user.

Selenium tests against AJAX applications

Web applications today are being designed in such a way that they appear the same as desktop applications. Web developers are accomplishing this by using AJAX within their web applications. **AJAX** stands for **Asynchronous JavaScript And XML** due to the fact that it relies on JavaScript creating asynchronous calls and then returning XML with the data that the user or application requires to carry on. AJAX does not rely on XML anymore, as more and more people move over **JSON, JavaScript Object Notation**, which is more lightweight in the way that it transfers the data. It does not rely on the extra overhead of opening and closing tags that is needed to create valid XML.

Time for action – working on pages with AJAX

In our first example, we are going to click on a link and then assert some text is visible on the screen:

1. Start up Selenium IDE and make sure that the Record button is pressed.

2. Navigate to `http://book.theautomatedtester.co.uk/chapter1`.

3. Click on the text that says **Click this link to load a page with AJAX**.

4. Verify the text that appears on your screen. Your test should look like the following screenshot:

5. Run the test that you have created. When it has finished running it should look like the following screenshot:

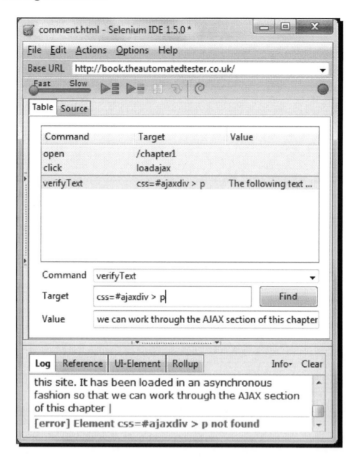

Have a look at the page that you are working against. Can you see the text that the test is expecting? You should see it, so why has this test failed? The test has failed because when the test reached that point, the element containing the text was not loaded into the DOM. This is because it was being requested and rendered from the web server into the browser.

To remedy this issue, we will need to add a new command to our test so that our tests pass in the future:

1. Right-click on the step that failed so the Selenium IDE context menu appears.

2. Click on **Insert New Command**.

3. In the **Command** select box, type **waitForElementPresent** or select it from the drop-down menu.

4. In the **Target** box add the target that is used in the **verifyText** command.

5. Run the test again and it should pass this time:

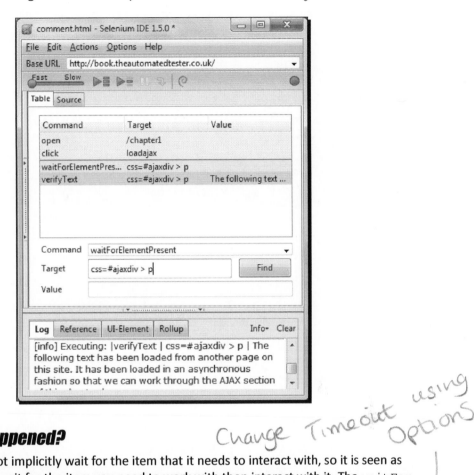

What just happened?

Selenium does not implicitly wait for the item that it needs to interact with, so it is seen as good practice to wait for the item you need to work with then interact with it. The `waitFor` commands will timeout after 30 seconds by default but if you need it to wait longer you can specify the tests by using the `setTimeout` command. This will set the timeout value that the tests will use in future commands.

Change Timeout using Options

If need be you can change the default wait if you go to **Options | Options** and then on the **General** tab and under **Default timeout** value of recorded command in milliseconds (30s = 30000ms) change it to what you want. Remember that there are 1000 milliseconds in a second.

Time for action – working with AJAX applications

As more and more applications try to act like desktop applications we need to be able to handle synchronization steps between our test and our application. In this section we will see how to handle AJAX and what to synchronize.

1. Click on the **load text to the page button.**

2. Navigate to `http://book.theautomatedtester.co.uk/chapter1`.

3. Wait for the text **I have been added with a timeout.** Your test will look like the following screenshot:

What just happened?

In the previous examples, we waited for an element to appear on the page; there are a number of different commands that we can use to wait. Also remember that we can take advantage of waiting for something not to be on the page. For example, `waitForElementNotPreset`. This can be just as effective as waiting for it to be there. The following commands make up the `waitFor` set of commands but this is not an exhaustive list:

- ◆ waitForAlertNotPresent
- ◆ waitForAlertPresent
- ◆ waitForElementPresent
- ◆ waitForElementNotPresent
- ◆ waitForTextPresent
- ◆ waitForTextNotPresent
- ◆ waitForPageToLoad
- ◆ waitForFrameToLoad

A number of these commands are run implicitly when other commands are being run. An example of this is the clickAndWait command. This will fire off a click command and then fire off a waitForPageToLoad. Another example is the open command which only completes when the page has fully loaded.

If you are feeling confident then it would be a good time to try different waitFor techniques.

Pop quiz – waiting for elements

1. If an element got added after the page has loaded what command would you use to make sure the test passed in the future?

 a. waitForElementPresent

    b. pause

    c. assertElementPresent

Storing information from the page in the test

Sometimes there is a need to store elements that are on the page to be used later in a test. This could be that your test needs to pick a date that is on the page and use it later so that you do not need to hardcode values into your test.

Once the element has been stored you will be able to use it again by requesting it from a JavaScript dictionary that Selenium keeps track of. To use the variable it will take one of the following two formats: it can look like ${variableName} or storedVars['variableName']. I prefer the storedVars format as it follows the same format as it is within Selenium internals.

Time for action – storing elements from the page

To see how this works lets work through the follow example:

1. Open up Selenium IDE and switch off the Record button.

2. Navigate to `http://book.theautomatedtester.co.uk/chapter1`.

3. Right-click on the text **Assert that this text is on the page** and go to the `storeText` command in the context menu and click on it.

4. A dialog will appear as shown in the following screenshot. Enter the name of a variable that you want to use. I have used **textOnThePage** as the name of my variable.

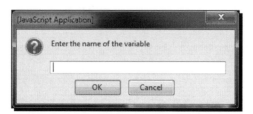

5. Click on the row below the `storeText` command in Selenium IDE.

6. Type `type` into the **Command** textbox.

7. Type `storeinput` into the **Target** box.

8. Type `${textOnThePage}` into the **Value** box.

9. Run the test. It should look like the following screenshot:

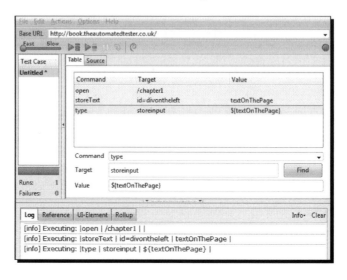

What just happened?

Once your test has completed running you will see that it has placed **Assert that this text is on the page** into the textbox.

Debugging tests

We have successfully created a number of tests and have seen how we can work against AJAX applications but unfortunately creating tests that run perfectly first time can be difficult. Sometimes, as a test automator, you will need to debug your tests to see what is wrong.

To work through this part of the chapter you will need to have a test open in Selenium IDE.

Time for action – debugging tests

These two steps are quite useful when your tests are not running and your want to execute a specific command.

1. Highlight a command.
2. Press the *X* key, this will make the command execute in Selenium IDE.

What just happened?

When a test is running you can press the **Pause** button to pause the test after the step that is currently being run. Once the test has been paused the **Step** button is no longer disabled and you can press it to step through the test as if you were stepping through an application.

If you are having issues with elements on the page you can type in their location and then click on the **Find** button. This will surround the element that you are looking for with a green border that flashes for a few seconds. It should look like the following screenshot:

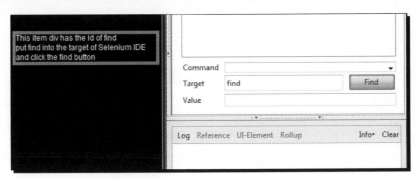

The echo command is also a good way to write something from your test to the log. This is equivalent to `Console.log in JavaScript`. For example, `echo | ${variableName}`.

Also remember that if you are trying to debug a test script that you have created with Selenium IDE, you can set breakpoints in your test. You simply right-click on the line and select breakpoint from the list. It will be similar to the following screenshot:

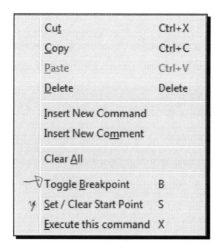

You can also use the keyboard shortcut of *B* to allow you to do it quicker.

Test Suites

We have managed to create a number of tests using Selenium IDE and have managed to run them successfully. The next thing to have a look at is how to create a test suite, so that we can open the test suite and then have it run a number of tests that we have created.

Time for action – creating Test Suites

If you have Selenium IDE open from the last steps, click on the **File** menu:

1. Click **New Test Case**.
2. You will see that Selenium IDE has opened a new area on the left of the IDE as shown in the following screenshot:

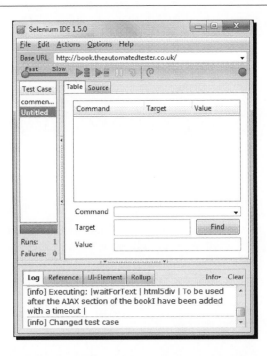

You can do this as many times as you want and when the **Play entire test suite** button is clicked it will run all the tests in the test suite. It will log all the passes and failures at the bottom of the Test Case box.

To **Save** this, click on the **File** menu and then click **Save Test Suite** and save the **Test Suite** file to somewhere that you can get to again. One thing to note is that saving a test suite does not save the test case. Make sure that you save the test case every time you make a change and not just the test suite.

To change the name of the test case to something a lot more meaningful you can do this by right-clicking on the test and clicking on the **Properties** item in the context menu:

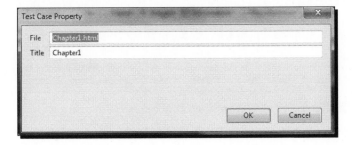

You can now add meaningful names to your tests and they will appear in Selenium IDE instead of falling back to their filenames.

What just happened?

We have managed to create our first test suite. This can be used to group tests together to be used later. If your tests have been saved, you can update the test suite properties to give the tests a name that is easier to read.

Pop quiz – Test Suites

1. How do we run all the tests in a test suite? *Right click on Test Case & click 'run test from here' or Play Entire test suite button.*

Saving tests

Saving tests is done in the same manner as saving a test suite. Click on the **File Menu** and then click **Save Test Case**. This will give you a save dialog, save this to somewhere that you can get to it later. When you save your tests and your test suite, Selenium IDE will try to keep the relationships between the folders in step when saving the tests and the test suites.

What you cannot record

We have seen our tests work really well by recording them and then playing them back. Unfortunately there are a number of things that Selenium cannot do. Since Selenium was developed in JavaScript, it tries to synthesize what the user does with JavaScript events. Unfortunately this does mean that it is bound by the same rules that JavaScript has in any browsers by operating within the sandbox.

- Silverlight and Flex/Flash applications, at the time of writing, cannot be recorded with Selenium IDE. Both these technologies operate in their own sandbox and do not operate with the DOM to do their work.

- HTML 5, at the time of writing, is not fully supported with Selenium IDE. A good example of this is elements that have the `contentEditable=true` attribute. If you want to see this, you can use the `type` command to type something into the `html5div` element. The test will tell you that it has completed the command but the UI will not have changed, as shown in the following screenshot:

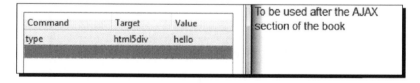

so no good for optimal sort

◆ Selenium IDE does not work with Canvas elements on the page either so you will not be able to make your tests move items around on a page.

◆ Selenium cannot do file uploads. This is due to the JavaScript sandbox not allowing JavaScript to interact with `<input type=file>` elements on a page. While you might be able to send the text to the box it will not always do what you expect, so I would recommend not doing it.

We will be able to automate a number of these elements with Selenium WebDriver in later chapters of this book.

Summary

We learnt a lot in this chapter about Selenium IDE, learning how to create your first test using the record and replay and understanding some of the basic concepts like moving between multiple windows that can appear in a test, and to save our tests for future use.

Specifically, we covered:

◆ **How to install Selenium IDE**: We started by downloading Selenium IDE from `http://seleniumhq.org`.

◆ **What Selenium IDE is made up of**: The breakup of Selenium IDE allowed us to see what makes up Selenium IDE. It allowed us to understand the different parts that make up a command that will be executed in a test as well as its basic format. We had a look at how to load Selenium IDE and how to get started with recording of tests. We saw that a Selenium IDE command is made up of three sections: the command, the target, and the value that might be used.

◆ **Recording and Replaying Tests**: We used Selenium IDE to record a workflow that a user will need in their tests. We also had a look at verifying and asserting that elements are on the page and that the text we are expecting is also on the page.

◆ **How to add comments to tests**: In this section of the chapter we saw how to add comments to the tests so that they are more maintainable.

◆ **Working with Multiple Windows**: Applications today can have pop-up windows that tests need to be able to move between.

◆ **Working with AJAX applications**: AJAX applications do not have the items needed for the tests when the tests get to commands. To get around this we had a look at adding `waitFor` commands to the tests. This is due to the fact that Selenium does not implicitly wait for elements to appear in the page.

- **Storing information in variables**: There is always something that is on the page that needs to be used later but unfortunately you will not know what the value is before the test runs. This section showed us how we can record items into a variable and use it later in a test. This could be something that has happened on a page and needs to check that it is still there on later pages.

- **Debugging tests**: Creating tests does not always go according to plan, so in this section we saw some of the different ways to debug your tests.

- **Saving Test Suites**: Finally we saw how we can save tests for future use and we can save them into different groups by saving them into test suites.

We also discussed what cannot be tested using Selenium IDE. We saw that Silverlight and Flex/Flash applications could not be tested, and that when working with a number of HTML 5 elements the tests say that they have completed the tasks even though the UI has not changed. In later chapters we will discuss different mechanisms that we can use within our tests that might be useful against HTML5 elements on the page.

Now that we've learnt about Selenium IDE, we're ready to look at all the different techniques to find elements on the page—which is the topic of the next chapter.

2
Locators

Locators allow us to find elements on a page that can be used in our tests. In the last chapter we managed to work against a page which had decent locators. In HTML, it is seen as good practice to make sure that every element you need to interact with has an ID attribute and a Name attribute. Unfortunately, following best practices can be extremely difficult to do, especially when building the HTML dynamically on the server before sending it back to the browser.

In this chapter we shall:

- Locate elements by ID
- Locate elements by Name
- Locate elements by Link
- Locate elements by XPath
- Locate elements by CSS
- Locate elements by DOM

So let's get on with it...

Locate by Id or name attribute + attribute value if needed)

Important preliminary points

Before starting this chapter we should begin by making sure that we have all the relevant applications installed. While these are not foolproof, they will give us some clue how to construct the locator for our tests to use.

- **Firebug**: `https://addons.mozilla.org/firefox/addon/firebug`

  Firebug has become the defacto tool for web developers as it allows developers to find elements on the page by using the find functionality.

  It has a JavaScript REPL. **REPL** stands for **Read-Eval-Print-Loop** or interactive shell that allows you to run JavaScript without having to create an entire page.

- **Firefinder**: `https://addons.mozilla.org/firefox/addon/firefinder-for-firebug`

  A very good tool for testing out XPath and CSS on the page. It will highlight all elements on the page that match the selector to your element location.

- **IE Developer Tools**:

  This is built into IE7, IE8 and IE9 that we can launch by pressing F12. It also has a number of features that Firebug has.

- **Google Chrome Developer Tools**:

  This, like IE, is built into the browser and will also allow you to find the elements on the page and be able to work out its XPath.

Once you have worked out your locator, you will need to put it into Selenium IDE to test it. At the beginning of *Chapter 1, Getting Started with Selenium IDE* there was a section that explained the layout of Selenium IDE. One of the buttons on the page is named **Find**. Click on this button when you have something in the **Value** textbox; it will highlight the item in green as shown in the next screenshot. On Mac OS X, the background color will flash yellow.

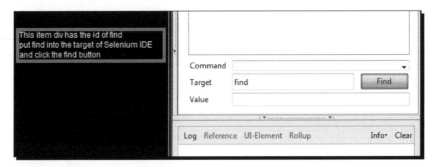

Now that we have these tools and understand how to use them we can start adding decent locators to our test scripts.

Locating elements by ID

On web applications today, elements should have an ID attribute for all their controls on the page. A control would be an element that we can interact with and is not static text. This allows Selenium to find the unique item, since IDs should be unique, and then complete the action that it needs to do against that element.

Time for action - finding IDs of elements on the page with Firebug

In this section we are going to find a number of elements that are on the page. You will need to have Firebug installed for this. We are going to look at how to find the ID of an element using Firefox.

1. Navigate to `http://book.theautomatedtester.co.uk/chapter2` and click on the Firebug icon.

2. Click on the Select Element icon in Firebug .

3. Move your mouse over the element that you wish to have a look at.

4. Move your mouse over different elements. As you can see in the following screenshot, firebug will highlight each of the items that you want to see:

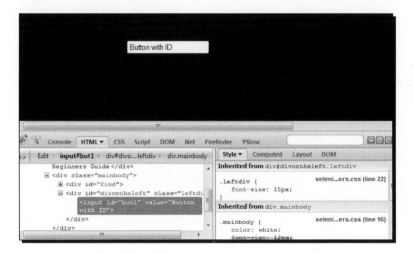

What just happened?

Once one has been selected, you can see that the element and all of the different attributes are now visible. We saw that the item became highlighted, or a single color box surrounded it, so that we can see which item is selected. We see this in the previous screenshot.

Now that we are confident on how to find elements and their attributes, let's start using them in Selenium.

Pop quiz – using the Find button

1. What color is an element bordered with when the **Find** button is clicked in Selenium IDE?

    a. Red

    b. Green

    c. Amber

    d. Yellow

Time for action - finding elements by ID

Elements often have IDs that are used to locate them. In the **Target** textbox this would look like `id=Element`. Follow the given example to see how it would work:

1. Open Selenium IDE.

2. Navigate to `http://book.theautomatedtester.co.uk/chapter2` and click on the Firebug icon.

3. Find any element that you want to interact with on the page and in the **Target** textbox of Selenium IDE, place its ID attribute value. Make sure that it has an ID attribute. For example, use **but1** as in the previous screenshot against `http://book.theautomatedtester.co.uk/chapter2`.

4. Type the command `click` into the **Command** selectbox.

5. Play your script.

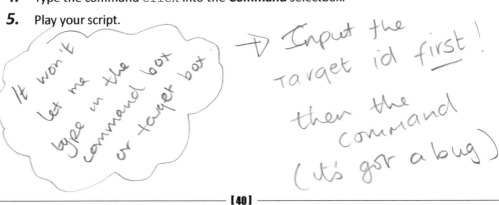

It won't let me type in the command box or target box

→ Input the target id first! then the command (it's got a bug)

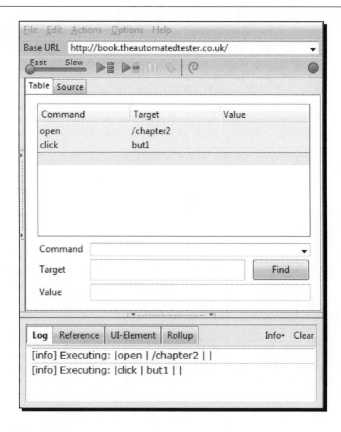

What just happened?

Your test will have executed the step successfully. Since the test is using the ID of the element, if that element were to be moved around, it would find the item without any issue. This is one of the main plus points of Selenium over a lot of the competing test frameworks out there.

Moving elements on the page

As I just mentioned, Selenium, when using the value of the ID attribute, can find the elements on the page even if they were moved. Click on the button with the text Random on the Chapter 2 page of the site (you can do this manually), and then run the script that we created earlier. You will see that your test executes successfully.

Time for action - finding elements by name

Elements do not necessarily have ID attributes on all of them. Elements can have names that we can use to locate them. In the Target textbox this would look like name=Element. Follow the given example to see how it would work:

1. Open Selenium IDE.

2. Navigate to http://book.theautomatedtester.co.uk/chapter2 and click on the Firebug icon.

3. Find any element that you want to interact with and in the Target textbox of Selenium IDE, place the value of its name attribute. For example, use **but2** as in the following screenshot against http://book.theautomatedtester.co.uk/chapter2.

4. Type the command `click` into the **Command** selectbox.

5. Play your script.

What just happened?

Your test will have executed the step successfully. Since the test is using the name of the element, if that element were to be moved around, it would find the item without any issue.

Adding filters to the name

There are times when there may be elements on the page that have the same name but a different attribute. When this happens we can apply filters to the locator so that Selenium IDE can find the element that we are after.

An example of this on the page would be `name=verifybutton value=chocolate;`. This will find the second button with the name `verifybutton`. See an example of this in the following screenshot:

Time for action - finding elements by link text

Probably the most common element on a page is a link. Links allow pages to be joined together so end users can navigate your site with confidence. You can see a screenshot of the element being found in Selenium IDE.

1. To specify that you want to follow a link you would use the target `link=link`.

2. On `http://book.theautomatedtester.co.uk/chapter2`, there is a link to the index page of the site. In the **Target** textbox in Selenium IDE, we are going to need to add `link=Index`. If you click **Find** button on Selenium IDE you will see the following:

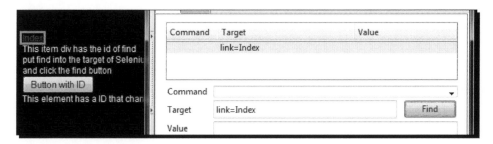

What just happened?

We have seen how we can find links that are on that page so that they can be used in your test. All that is needed is the inner text of the nodes in the DOM.

Time for action - finding elements by accessing the DOM via JavaScript

There are times where the DOM will be updated via AJAX and this means that our locator needed for the test will need some form of JavaScript to see if it is there. In JavaScript, calling the DOM to find the first link on the page would look like `document.links[0];`. `document` represents the HTML document and `links` is an array on that object. On the Chapter 2 page of the website, it will show the link that we used in the previous section of this chapter.

But normally it will just be calls to the DOM to see if an element has been added like in the following screenshot:

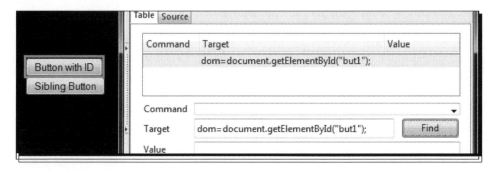

What just happened?

We have just seen that we can use JavaScript to find elements on the page. This can be extremely useful if you have a web application that does a lot of interaction with the DOM.

Read again

Pop quiz – finding Elements with DOM JavaScript

1. If you wanted to use JavaScript to find the element on the page, which strategy would you use to find it?

    a. ID

    b. Name

    c. DOM

    d. CSS Selector

    e. XPath

Read again.

Time for action – finding elements by XPath

Unfortunately, best practices cannot always be followed when building the markup or if they are, then they may have a dynamic edge to them. An example of this would be working against a page that uses a key from the database as the element ID, so when something is edited and stored back in the database it can be found a lot quicker and updated. In this section of the chapter, we are going to work with XPath. XPath allows us to query the DOM as though it were an XML document. With XPath we can do some rather complex queries to find elements on the page that may not have been accessible otherwise.

Let's start by creating a basic XPath. We are going to look for an input button:

1. Open Selenium IDE.

2. Navigate to `http://book.theautomatedtester.co.uk/chapter2`.

3. Type `click` into the **Command** selectbox.

4. Type `xpath=//input` into the **Target** textbox.

5. Click on the **Find** button. It will find a button on the page like in the following screenshot. Note that sometimes Selenium IDE will flash the button yellow:

What just happened?

Your test will have looked against the DOM to find an element that was of the type input. The `xpath=` at the beginning tells Selenium that the element needed will be located by XPath. It removes the guess work that Selenium would have to do and is seen as good practice. The `//` tells the query that it needs to stop at the first element that it finds. It is a greedy query so if you have a rather large web page, it can take some time to return since it will try to parse the page. Writing the XPath like this allows us to make changes to the UI, within reason, and not have it impact the test.

Using direct XPath in your test

As I mentioned in the first part of this section, having `//` as the start of your XPath is seen as a greedy query since it will parse the entire DOM until it finds the element that you want to find. If you want to work against an element that will always be in a certain place, you can use a more direct XPath.

Time for action – finding elements by direct XPath

Instead of using the `//`, you can use a single `/` but you will need to make sure that the first node in your query is HTML. Let's see an example of this:

1. Open Selenium IDE.

2. Navigate to `http://book.theautomatedtester.co.uk/chapter2`.

3. Type `xpath=/html/body/div[2]/div[3]/input` into the **Target** input of Selenium IDE.

4. Click on the **Find** button.

What just happened?

The previous locator will have found the same element as before. This type of XPath query will find the element fractionally quicker but if your UI is going to change, it may fail if the element is moved into a different area of the page. One thing to really note is that XPath locators can be extremely fragile. They can find what you want but the slightest change to your HTML and they break, meaning that you need to do maintenance on that test. I would recommend only using these if you have to.

You will have noticed that parent and child nodes are in the same query. Since HTML has a tree structure, it just notifies the query that it needs to start at the html node, then move to its child node, body, then to body's child, and so on until it reaches the end of the query. Once it has done that it will stop executing the query.

Using XPath to find the nth element of a type

There are a lot of occasions where as a Selenium user you will have to click on an edit button in a table so that you can update something specific. Have a look at the button that you wish to click; it does not have a unique name or ID. An example of this is the button with the value "Sibling Button".

When doing a query against the DOM, an array of elements is returned to Selenium that match the query. For example if you were to do //div on the Chapter 2 page of the website, there are three elements returned to Selenium. If your test is only relying on the first item in your test, then it will try and access only the first item. If you wanted to interact with the second element then your query would look like //div[2]. Note that the second to nth element need to be sibling nodes of the first element that is returned. If they are not and you were to access the element it would fail saying that it could not find them.

We can see this with the input buttons that are present on the page. They all reside in their own containing div element, so do not have any sibling elements that are also input elements. If you were to put //input[2] into Selenium IDE, it would not be able to find the element and fail.

You can see an example of this in the following screenshot:

Using element attributes in XPath queries

There are times that you will need to find elements that are the same except for the difference in one or two attributes. To handle this we can add the attributes to the query so that we can try to make the element more unique for use in the test. The format can be used for any attribute on any element. It will always follow `xpath=//element[@ attribute='attribute value']`. For example, if you have two `div` elements on the page, but they only differ by the class attribute, your XPath query would look like the following: `xpath=//div[@class='classname']`.

Try doing this with Selenium yourself by trying to identify something unique about the `div` elements on the page. When you have completed the task your query should look like one of the following in the next screenshot:

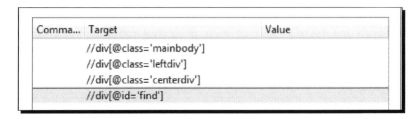

Doing a partial match on attribute content

As mentioned earlier there are times where there is no way for a developer to create a static ID for elements on the page. This could be down to the fact that the element is being loaded asynchronously via AJAX or because it is using the key of the data as it is stored in the database.

There are times where only part of the ID is dynamic. This is to allow the developer to cram more information onto the page so that the user has everything they need. We will need to have a mechanism to work with these elements.

To do the partial match, your query will need to have the word `contains` with the attribute and the partial match that it needs. For example, if you wanted to access the element that has the text in it "This element has an ID that changes every time the page is loaded", you will use `//div[contains(@id, 'time_')]`. This is due to the first part of the ID always being static. The locator could also use `starts-with` instead of `contains` to make the XPath query stricter in what is returned. The queries in the following screenshot will find the same element on the page:

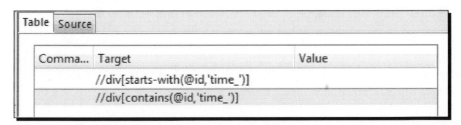

Finding an element by the text it contains

Finding elements by the text they contain can be quite useful when working with web pages that have been created dynamically. The elements could be from using a web based WYSIWYG editor or you might just like to find a paragraph on the page with specific text to then do further queries on.

To do this your query will need to have the `text()` method call in the query. It will match the entire contents of the node if it has the format `//element[text()='inner text']`. As seen in the previous section, your query can use the `contains` keyword to allow it to have a bit more leniency to what it finds. Next you can find a screenshot of queries that will find the same element as the previous section:

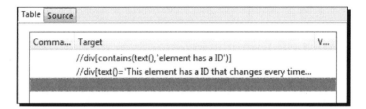

Using XPath Axis to find elements

As we have seen, XPath is normally only used if the element we need to interact with is not accessible by normal means. In this section of the chapter, we are going to have a look at leveraging XPath Axis in our queries to find the element that we wish to interact with.

An example that I have used in the real world was to find a table cell that had specific text, then traverse the tree backwards to find the edit button so that I could click on it. This may seem like an extreme example just to click on an edit button but is extremely common according to the Selenium Users forum on Google Groups.

Time For Action – using XPath Axis

In the first example, we are going to find a button and then find its sibling. In this example, the query that we will generate is equivalent to `xpath=//div[@class='leftdiv']/input[2]`.

1. We will start by finding the first element for our query which is `//input[@value='Button with ID']`. Place that into Selenium IDE Target textbox and see which element it highlights.

2. There is another button below the one that is highlighted and that is the element that we need to work with in this section. The button is the next input item in the HTML, so it is elements `following-sibling` that we need. Our locator will look like `//input[@value='Button with ID']/following-sibling::input[@value='Sibling Button']` and if it was placed into Selenium IDE it would be able to find the element that we are after; see the following screenshot:

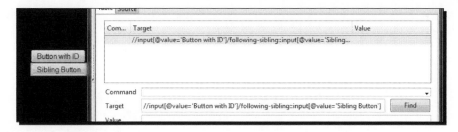

What just happened?

We have just seen how we can use XPath axis to find the elements that we need in our tests. We managed to find the element using the following-sibling axis.

As mentioned earlier you can use XPath to find an element and then walk backwards up the tree. If we were to take the example that we have just done and reverse it, you will need to start at the button with the value **Sibling Button** and then go back to the button with the value **Button with ID** the XPath query would then look like.

We can see it finding the element in the following screenshot:

Following is a list of Axis that you can use in your XPath queries to find the elements on the page:

Axis name	Result
ancestor	Selects all the ancestors (parent, grandparent, and so on) of the element
descendant	Selects all the descendants (children, grandchildren, and so on) of the element
following	Selects all elements that follow the closing tab of the current element
following-sibling	Selects all the siblings after the current element
parent	Selects the parent of the current element
preceding	Selects all elements that are before the current element
preceding-Sibling	Selects all of the siblings before the current element

As we have seen, there is a large number of different ways to find the same element on the web page. Having XPath queries in your test can be really useful for finding elements on the page but can slow down your test. Browsers like Internet Explorer 6 do not have built-in XPath libraries and rely on doing the XPath query via JavaScript which can mean that a test that uses XPath can run two or more times slower than a test with IDs. The more complex the XPath, the slower the test since it needs to do more DOM traversals which is an expensive operation.

There is also another way to do XPath-like queries against the DOM and use built-in libraries in most browsers. We can use CSS selectors which is the next section of this book.

Pop quiz – using XPath Axis

1. Pick two from the following if you wanted do a partial match on an attribute on an element from the beginning of the value:

    a. `contains()`

    b. `starts-with()`

    c. `ends-with()`

Have a go hero – working with XPath Axis

Go to `http://financial-dictionary.thefreedictionary.com/` and use `contains()`, `starts-with()`, and `ends-with()` on the page. Use the call `getXPathCount()` to see how many items you can get with your XPath query.

CSS selectors

We saw in the previous section that XPath selectors can offer your tests a lot of flexibility to find elements on the page.

It must be noted that Selenium IDE and Selenium RC uses Sizzle, the framework used for selectors in jQuery, to find elements on the page. Not all of these can be translated to work in Selenium WebDriver. When we come across items like this, it will be mentioned in that section.

Time for action - finding elements by CSS

So, finding elements by XPath can be an extremely costly exercise. A way around this is to use CSS selectors to find the objects that you need. Selenium is compatible with CSS 1.0, CSS 2.0, and CSS 3.0 selectors. There are a number of items that are supported like namespace in CSS 3.0 and some pseudo classes and pseudo elements.

The syntax of your locator will look like `css=cssSelector`. Let's create our first selector to find an element on our page.

1. Open Selenium IDE.

2. Navigate to `http://book.theautomatedtester.co.uk/chapter2` and click on the Firebug icon. Click on the **Firefinder** tab in Firebug.

3. We are going to look at one of the buttons in the `div` with the ID `divontheleft`. The CSS Selector for the buttons would be `div.leftdiv input`. Place that into FireFinder and click on the **Filter** button.

4. Your browser should show something like the following screenshot:

5. If you were now to put this into Selenium IDE , insert `css=div.leftdiv` input into the **Target** textbox and click on the **Find** button, it should look like the next screenshot. You can also write this as `div[class='leftdiv']` in Firefinder to make it look similar to XPath:

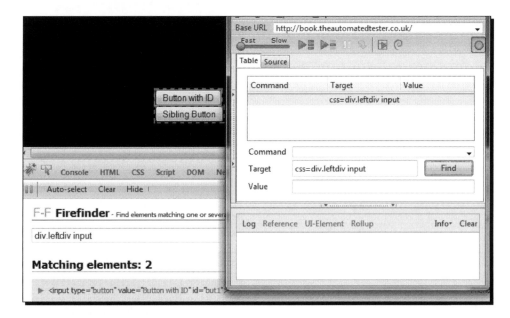

What just happened?

We have seen how Selenium has used the same CSS selector to find a button. Unlike in normal CSS, Selenium is only interested in the first element that matches the query and that is why in the second picture only the first button was highlighted and not its sibling.

Using child nodes to find the element

In the previous example we saw that we were able to find the input button that was a child of the `div` node in the DOM. `div.leftdiv input` will look for the `div` and then look for an input node in the DOM that is below that. It looks for any descendant that will match. This is the equivalent to using `descendant` in your XPath query.

If we needed to look for the child of the element we would have to place > between the `div` selector and the input selector. Your locator would look like `css=div.leftdiv > input` or `css=div.leftdiv input`. In the case of the Chapter 2 page of the website, both will work as they are direct children of `div.leftdiv`.

Using sibling nodes to find the element

Finding elements by using a sibling node in the DOM is probably the most common way to access an element. In the XPath section of the book, we saw that we could use the `following-sibling` operator in the XPath Query. The equivalent CSS Selector syntax is a + between DOM nodes in the query. It will check its direct next node to see if it matches until it finds the element. So working against the HTML, we will create a CSS selector to find the second input button:

```
<div id="divontheleft" class="leftdiv">
   <input id='but1' value='Button with ID' type='button'/>
   <br/>
   <input value='Sibling Button' type='button'/>
</div>
```

`css=input#but1` will find the first button and then its sibling is the `br` and its sibling is `input`. The final selector will look like this: `css=input#but1 + br + input`. You can see this in the following screenshot of Selenium IDE:

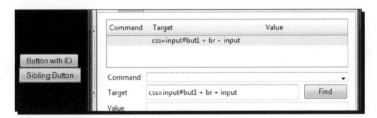

Using CSS class attributes in CSS selectors

Finding elements by their CSS class is going to be the most common method. A lot of the queries that people create start with a containing node distinguishing it by the CSS class and then moving through the DOM to a child or grandchild node to find the element that you wish to work again. The syntax for finding the item is to put the node, like a `div`, then put a dot, and then the class. For example, to find the `div` with the class `centerdiv` it would look like this: `css=div.centerdiv`.

Using element IDs in CSS selectors

As we saw in XPath queries there are times when we need to find the element that is next to an element that we know the ID of. This means that we can access a lot more of the DOM, and since it is a CSS selector there is a good chance that it will be a lot faster than its XPath equivalent.

To find an element by ID in a CSS selector we need to place a # in front of the ID of the element in the CSS selector. For example, if we wanted to find a `div` with the ID of `divinthecenter`, the CSS selector would look like this: `css=div#divinthecenter`. You can also simplify this down to `css=#divinthecenter`. This is due to IDs on elements having to be unique.

If you were to place this in the **Target** textbox of Selenium IDE and click **Find**, it should highlight the item as in the following screenshot:

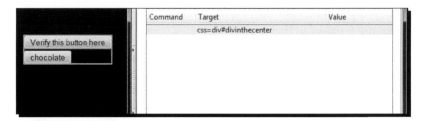

Finding elements by their attributes

In the *Using element attributes in XPath queries* section, we saw how useful it could be to find an element by looking at their attributes. It could be that an element may have the same name but a different value, so finding them according to their attributes can be extremely powerful. In this example, we are going to look for the button that has the value chocolate. On web page buttons, a value is what is displayed on the screen.

The syntax for looking at the attribute is `node[attribute='value']`. So in the case of the button with the value chocolate, it will be `input[value='chocolate']`. If you were to put that into Selenium IDE, it will have the format `css=input[value='chocolate']` and when you click the **Find** button you will see the same as shown in the following screenshot:

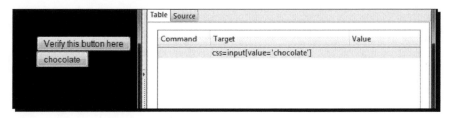

Another example of this is if you were trying to find an element according to its `href`. The syntax for that would be `a[href='path']`. You can try this on the Index page and try and find the link to this chapter. When you have done it, it should look something like `css=a[href='/chapter2']`. If you click the **Find** button, it will highlight the Chapter 2 link.

Chaining of attributes is also supported in Selenium to make sure that your test is using one specific element on the page. The syntax will be `css=node[attr1='value1'][attr2='value2']`. An example on the page that we are working against would be `css=input[id='but1'][value='Button with ID']`; this will find the button with the value **Button with ID**. You can chain as many attributes as you want in this manner.

Partial matches on attributes

In XPath queries we saw that we could use `contains` to find partial matches of values to attributes. This can be extremely useful for locating elements based on part of their ID if it is dynamically generated. Following is a table explaining the different syntax needed and after that we have a look at some working examples:

Syntax	Description
^=	Finds the item starting with the value passed in. This is the equivalent to the XPath `starts-with`.
$=	Finds the item ending with the value passed in. This is the equivalent to the XPath `ends-with`.
*=	Finds the item which matches the attribute that has the value that partially matches. This is equivalent to the XPath `contains`.

In the XPath section of this chapter, we had a look at the XPath `//div[contains(@id, 'time_')]` which has a dynamic ID. The equivalent CSS selector would be `div[id^='time_']` or `div[id*='time_']`. The following screenshot shows both of the selectors highlighting the element we want:

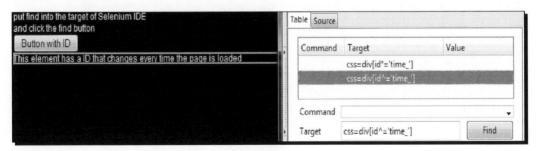

Time for action – finding the nth element with CSS

There are times where we need to find the nth element after a parent element on the page. In the XPath examples, we looked at the second input after the div with the class leftdiv. The XPath looked like this: xpath=//div[@class='leftdiv']/input[2]. To find the second to nth element we will need to use pseudo classes. Pseudo classes are used to add special effects to selectors. In this case we are going to use :nth-child for the first example.

1. Open Selenium IDE.

2. Navigate to http://book.theautomatedtester.co.uk/chapter2.

3. Type css=div#divinthecenter *:nth-child(3). This will find the same as xpath=//div[@class='leftdiv']/input[2].

4. Click on the **Find** button.

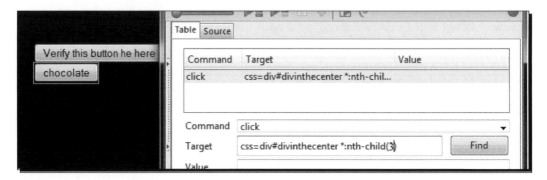

What just happened?

Unfortunately Selenium does not support the :nth-of-type pseudo class, so you will not be able to access the specific type. This pseudo class is extremely greedy in the way that it does look up over the page. It is also not available to the element selector library that is in use by Selenium. This is why the selector is using the wildcard * and then finding the nth-child from our starting div. The downside to using a selector in this manner is if any other node was placed in the way it would make the tests fail.

Finding an element by its inner text

Finding elements by their inner text can also be quite useful. In the XPath section of the book, we used the `text()` function to see the text it had. Earlier we had `xpath=//div[contains(text(),'element has a ID')]` to find a `div` with text in it. To update this XPath to a CSS Selector we would need to use the `:contains` pseudo class. This pseudo class is part of Sizzle which is used in Selenium IDE and Selenium RC. This will only work on browsers that do not have the CSS `querySelector` available. WebDriver delegates that task down to the browser if it can. I would recommend not using `:contains` if you plan on moving to Selenium WebDriver.

 It is important to know that CSS selectors only have a read forward process. This means that you cannot find an element and then traverse backwards up the DOM. This is what makes CSS selectors a lot faster than XPath queries to find the same elements.

Pop quiz – using locators

1. What is the most common way to find an element on a page?

    a. ID

    b. XPath

    c. CSS Selector

    d. Name

2. If you wanted to find the sibling input that is after an input in the DOM, what would the XPath look like?

3. What would the CSS look like for the previous question?

Have a go hero – working against Google Maps

Now that you have managed to create tests with different locators, try working against Google Maps. It is an extremely good site to work with XPath and CSS as it never has IDs or Names.

Summary

We learnt a lot in this chapter about locators. We have been able to use a large number of different methods to find the elements that are on a page. We have seen how to find elements using the easy methods like `id=`, `name=` to find elements and running queries against the DOM to find them using CSS selectors or XPath queries.

Specifically, we covered:

- **Using Firebug to find the element attributes**: In this section we were able to start using Firebug. This will become an invaluable tool for anyone that works with web applications. It has a very good mechanism for finding elements so you can work against them.

- **Finding an element by ID**: Elements can easily be found by the value of the ID attribute. This is the most common way to find elements and is the fastest way to find the elements on the page.

- **Finding an element by name**: When elements do not have the IDs but do have a name attribute your tests can use those.

- **Finding an element by DOM query**: In this section we were able to use the power of JavaScript DOM API calls to find the element that we wish to work with. This can be from the most basic call to the document to a JavaScript function that you can pass variables to.

- **Finding an element using XPath queries**: In this section we were able to find the element on the page by using XPath queries. Your test can use relative paths or even XPath functions to find the element on the page. The queries can be as complex as you want but remember that they can impact the speed of the test.

- **Finding an element using CSS selectors**: When XPath queries are making your tests run slow, especially in browsers that do not have good support for XPath. CSS selectors are starting to become the default way to find elements on web pages with popular JavaScript libraries, and there is not a large learning curve to get working with it.

We also discussed how XPath queries can make tests run slower on browsers that do not have native XPath support. Internet Explorer 6 is the main browser where you would see this issue. When tests start running extremely slowly with XPath, we can move our tests over to CSS to see large speed gains in our tests.

If locator does not have the locator type identifier in front of it, Selenium will default to the following strategies:

- ◆ DOM: For locators starting with document
- ◆ XPath: For locators starting with //
- ◆ Identifier: For any other locator using ID and name of the element

Now that we've learnt how to locate the elements on the page, we're ready to learn how WebDriver is made up—which is the topic of the next chapter.

3

Overview of Selenium WebDriver

In this chapter, we will have a look at the history of Selenium WebDriver from its inception to where it is currently. We will also have a look at the architecture of Selenium WebDriver so we can get a better understanding of how all the commands work.

We will finish the chapter by making sure that we have understood the history of Selenium WebDriver and also have a working understanding of how Selenium WebDriver is built.

In this chapter, we shall:

- Learn the history of Selenium WebDriver
- Architecture
- How to set up your Java environment

So let's get on with it...

Important preliminary points

In this chapter, we will be writing our tests in Java. This is down to the popularity of the language by people using Selenium as well as its support on multiple platforms. To do this we will need to have an IDE to write the tests in. I recommend using IDEA Intellij at `http://www.jetbrains.com/idea/download/` as it will give you all the tools that you need to build your tests successfully. You will also need to download JUnit from `https://github.com/KentBeck/junit/downloads`. This will allow us to drive the tests and do asserts during the tests.

We are also going to need to download the necessary files to allow us to use Selenium WebDriver with Java. We will need to download `selenium-server-<version>.zip` from `http://code.google.com/p/selenium/downloads/list`. The `<version>` will appear like `2.x.x` on the site.

History of Selenium

With web applications becoming the defacto approach to developing end user applications, a solution for testing is needed. This has meant more and more emphasis is needed on a browser automation framework to help with checking the site.

For years people have been using Selenium IDE and Selenium RC to drive a number of different types of browsers. Selenium, when originally created by Jason Huggins, solved the issue of getting the browser to do user interactions.

This is a good automation framework, however it is limited by the JavaScript sandbox in browsers. The JavaScript sandbox enforces security policies while JavaScript is executing to prevent malicious code executing on the client machine. The main security policy people come across is the Same Origin Policy. If you needed to move from HTTP to HTTPS, like you normally would during a log on process, the browser would block the action because we are no longer in the same origin. This was quite infuriating for your average developer!

The Selenium API was originally designed to work from within the server. The developer or tester writing the tests had to do so in HTML using a three column design based on the FIT. You can see how this looks if you open up Selenium IDE: the three input boxes that need to be completed for each line that will be executed. It has a number of issues in that you cannot do anything that you may do with a Turing complete language.

Patrick Lightbody and Paul Hammant thought that there must be a better way to drive their tests and in a way that they could use their favorite development language. They created Selenium Remote Control using Java as a web server that would proxy traffic. It would inject Selenium onto the page and then it would be used in a similar manner as to what it was in the three column manner. This also creates more of a procedural style of development.

The Selenium RC API for the programming languages that are supported have been designed to fit the original three column syntax. Commonly known as Selenese, it has grown over the life of the project to support the changes that have been happening to web applications. This has had the unfortunate consequence that the API has grown organically so that users can manipulate the browser the way they intend but still keep to the original three column syntax. There is somewhere in the region of 140 methods available which makes picking the right method for the job rather difficult.

With the move to mobile devices and HTML5, Selenium RC was starting to show that it wasn't able to fulfill its original requirement: browser automation to mimic what the user is doing.

Simon Stewart, having hit a number of these issues, wanted to try a different approach to driving the browser. While working for ThoughtWorks, he started working on the WebDriver project. It started originally as a way to drive HTMLUnit and Internet Explorer but having learnt lessons from Selenium RC, Simon was able to design the API to fit in with the way most developers think. Developers have been doing Object Orientated development for a while, so moving away from the procedural style of Selenium RC was a welcome change to developers. For those interested I suggest reading Simon Stewart's article on Selenium design at `http://www.aosabook.org/en/selenium.html`.

The next section will go through the basic architecture of WebDriver.

Architecture

The WebDriver architecture does not follow the same approach as Selenium RC, which was written purely in JavaScript for all the browser automation. The JavaScript, in Selenium RC, would then emulate user actions. This JavaScript would automate the browser from within the browser. WebDriver on the other hand tries to control the browser from outside the browser. It uses accessibility API to drive the browser. The accessibility API is used by a number of applications for accessing and controlling applications when they are used by disabled users and is common to web browsers.

WebDriver uses the most appropriate way to access the accessibility API. If we look at Firefox, it uses JavaScript to access the API. If we look at Internet Explorer, it uses C++. This approach means we can control browsers in the best possible way but has the downside that new browsers entering the market will not be supported straight away like we can with Selenium RC.

Where that approach doesn't work we will then inject JavaScript into the page. Examples of this are found in the new HTML5.

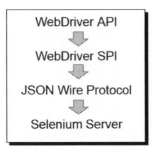

The system is made up of four different sections.

WebDriver API

The WebDriver API is the part of the system that you interact with all the time. Things have changed from the 140 line long API that the Selenium RC API had. This is now more manageable and can actually fit on a normal screen. You will see this when you start using WebDriver in the next chapter. This is made up of the WebDriver and the WebElement objects.

```
driver.findElement(By.name("q"))
```

and

```
element.sendKeys("I love cheese");
```

These commands are then translated to the SPI, which is stateless. This can be seen in the next section.

WebDriver SPI

When code enters the **Stateless Programming Interface** or **SPI**, it is then called to a mechanism that breaks down what the element is, by using a unique ID, and then calling a command that is relevant. All of the API calls above then call down.

Using the example in the previous section would be like the following code, once it was in the SPI:

```
findElement(using="name", value="q")
sendKeys(element="webdriverID", value="I love cheese")
```

From there we call the JSON Wire protocol. We still use HTTP as the main transport mechanism. We communicate to the browsers and have a simple client server transport architecture the WebDriver developers created the JSON Wire Protocol.

JSON Wire protocol

The WebDriver developers created a transport mechanism called the JSON Wire Protocol. This protocol is able to transport all the necessary elements to the code that controls it. It uses a REST like API as the way to communicate.

Selenium server

The Selenium server, or browser, depending on what is processing, uses the JSON Wire commands to break down the JSON object and then does what it needs to. This part of the code is dependent on which browser it is running on.

As mentioned earlier, it could be done in the browser via C++; if it's in IE or if not available we inject Selenium.

The merging of two projects

Both Simon Stewart and Jason Huggins thought that it would be a really good idea to merge the two projects together. This was then called Selenium 2.

The Selenium core developers have been working really hard to simplify the code base and remove as much duplication as possible. We have created what is known as Selenium Atoms which is then shared between the two projects.

Now that we know the basics of how it all hangs together, let us set up a project that we can use for the rest of the chapter.

How to set up your Java environment

All of the examples that follow in the book will be in Java. We need to make sure that we know how to set up the Java environment.

Time for action – setting up Intellij IDEA project

We will be setting up using JUnit as the testing framework to drive our tests.

1. Open IDEA and create a new project.

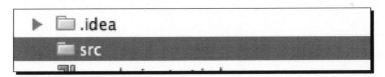

2. Create a directory at the root of the project called test using **New | Directory**.

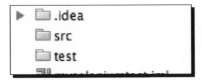

3. Click on **File | Project structure**.
4. Click on **Modules** on the left-hand side of the dialog that has loaded.

5. Click on the `test` folder that you created in the folder tree on the right-hand side of the dialog.

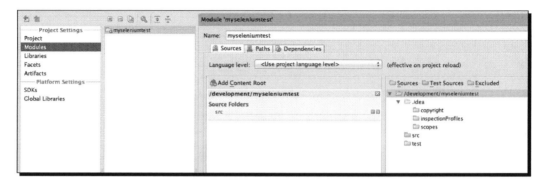

6. Click on the **Test Sources** button and the `test` folder should turn green. It will look like the following screenshot:

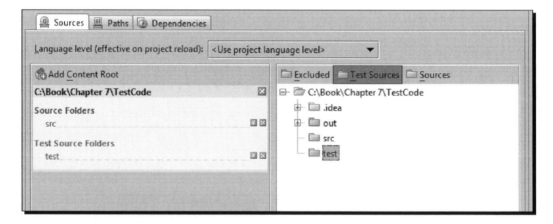

7. Click on **File | Project structure**.

8. Click on **Global libraries**.

9. Click on the **+** to add a **New Global library**. And then select **Java**.

10. Click on **Attach Classes** and add `selenium.jar` and `common.jar`. This should be in the same place as your `Selenium-Server.jar`. When added, it should look like the following screenshot:

11. Do the same for JUnit now. You can create a new **Global** library for it or add it to the **Selenium Global Library**.

12. Click on the **Modules** link on the left-hand side again.

13. Click on the **Dependencies** tab.

14. Click on **Add** and click on **Global Libraries**. Add the Selenium and JUnit libraries.

15. Click on **Apply**. When this is done the text `selenium` should turn purple.

16. We are now ready to run Selenium Server. We do this by running `java-jar` `selenium-server.jar` from a command prompt or from a terminal depending on your operating system.

Your project is ready to have tests added to it. Each of the files that we create from now on will be placed in the test directory and will be run when we need to.

What just happened?

We have successfully set up a project to Selenium WebDriver. When we are working through all of the chapters going forward we will know that they will have all the aspects needed.

Pop quiz – setting up the test project

1. Where will we be adding our tests that we create with Selenium WebDriver in Intellij?

Summary

We learnt a lot in this chapter about how Selenium and WebDriver were created and how they work together.

Specifically, we covered:

◆ **History**: In this section we learnt how Selenium came to being. Selenium WebDriver is the merger of two automation frameworks: Selenium and WebDriver.

◆ **Architecture**: We learnt how all of the different mechanisms work together to produce the framework that we will be using throughout this book.

◆ **Setting up a Java environment**: In this section we saw how we can run projects later on in the book.

Now that we've learnt the history and architecture of Selenium WebDriver, as well setting up our environment to create Java Projects, let us have a look at the design patterns we should use with Selenium WebDriver to make test creation easier, which is the topic of the next chapter.

4

Design Patterns

In this chapter we are going to have a look at good design patterns for creating maintainable and reusable bits of code that we can use with our Selenium tests. This means that if there are any changes needed to our web application or changes in the way we need to find elements, we can change it once and have it fix everything very quickly.

In this chapter, we shall learn:

◆ Page Object design

◆ Using Page Factory in Page Objects

◆ Using LoadableComponents

So let's get on with it...

Important preliminary points

In this chapter it will be assumed that all files will have the following `import` statements:

```
import org.openqa.selenium.By;
import org.openqa.selenium.WebDriver;
import org.openqa.selenium.WebElement;
import org.openqa.selenium.support.FindBy;
```

Page Objects

In this section of the chapter, we are going to have a look at how we can apply some best practices to tests. You will learn how to make maintainable test suites that will allow you to update tests in seconds. We will have a look at creating your own DSL so that people can see intent. We will create tests using the Page Object Pattern.

Let us start trying to put these best practices to work.

Time for action – setting up the test

Imagine that you have a number of tests that work on a site that requires you to log in and move to a certain page. Or imagine that you need to have a test that requires you to be on a certain page. In these two situations the quickest way to find out which page you are on and then move to the correct one if need be, is to start testing. This is to make sure that we follow one of the major tenants of test automation, in that you always start from a known place. Let us see this in an example:

Create a new Java class in IDEA:

1. Import the relevant Selenium Packages.

2. Create the `setup()` and `teardown()` method. I prefer the JUnit 4 style of tests and will show code samples with the annotations.

3. We need to check that the page is on the correct page. For this we will use the `selenium.getTitle` to see the page title and then if incorrect move to the chapter 2 link. We do this because navigating to page is slower than checking the page's title or any other calls to the page already loaded.

4. We need to then validate that it is correct and then work accordingly. The following is a code snippet of how we can do this:

```
if (!"Page 2".equals(selenium.getTitle())){
  selenium.get(
    "http://book.theautomatedtester.co.uk/chapter2");
}
```

5. Create the rest of the test to check that items are on the page.

What just happened?

We have just seen how we can check if something is what the test is expecting. If it is, the test will carry on as we expect. If it isn't what we expect, we can move our test to the correct page and then carry on with that page. We will see that if you log into the @Before, you may not start your tests.

Now let's have a look at how we can make more tests maintainable by splitting areas out into other methods.

Time for action – moving Selenium steps into private methods to make tests maintainable

Imagine that you just need to test one page on your site and you have quite a few tests for this page. A lot of the tests will be using the same code over and over again. This can be quite annoying to maintain if something changes on the page meaning we have to go through all the tests to fix this one issue. The way that we will fix this is to refactor the tests so they are simpler and therefore easier to read.

1. Let us create a number of tests as follows:

```
@Test
public void shouldCheckButtonOnChapter2Page(){
   selenium.get("http://book.theautomatedtester.co.uk");
   selenium.findElement(By.link, "Chapter2").click();
   Assert.assertEqual(selenium.findElements(
     By.id"but1").getSize(), 1);
}

@Test
public void shouldCheckAnotherButtonOnChapter2Page(){
   selenium.get("http://book.theautomatedtester.co.uk");
   selenium.findElement(By.link, "Chapter2").click();
   Assert.assertEqual(selenium.findElements(
     By.id, "verifybutton").getSize(), 1);

}
```

2. Using the previous examples, let's break these down.

3. In both the examples, we can see that it is always opening the root of the site. Let's move that into its own private method. To do this in IDEA, you highlight the lines you want to refactor and then right-click. Use the context menu and then the extract method.

4. Then you will see a dialog asking you to give the method a name. Give it something meaningful for the test. I have called it **loadHomePage** as you can see in the following screenshot:

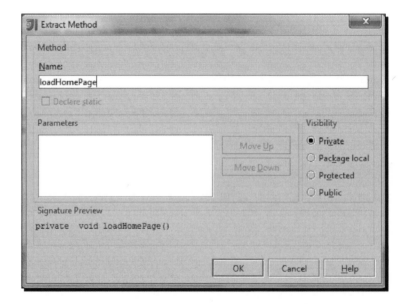

5. Now do the same for the other parts of the tests so that it makes the test look a lot more succinct.

6. Your test class should look something like this:

```
@Test
public void shouldCheckButtonOnChapter2Page(){
  loadHomePage();
```

```
  clickAndLoadChapter2();
  Assert.assertEquals(selenium.findElements(
    By.id("but1")).size(), 1);

@Test
public void shouldCheckAnotherButtonOnChapter2Page(){
  loadHomePage();
  clickAndLoadChapter2();
  Assert.assertEquals(selenium.findElements(
    By.id("verifybutton")).size(), 1);

private void loadHomePage() {
  selenium.get("http://book.theautomatedtester.co.uk");
}

private void clickAndLoadChapter2() {
  selenium.findElement(By.linkText("Chapter2")).click();
}
```

What just happened?

We have just started making our tests a lot more maintainable. We saw how we can break this down into more succinct and readable tests that show intent rather than showing a test as a clump of Selenium calls. This also makes the tests a lot more manageable because if I were to change the link on the root from "Chapter2" to "Chapter 2", I would need to only fix it in one place rather than *n* places where *n* is the number of times that sequence is in the test class.

Now let's have a look at how we can use the Page Object Pattern for creating a DSL over the site.

Time for action – using the Page Object Pattern to design tests

Imagine that you have a site that has a number of different pages that you need to test. This is quite common for a number of sites. We can create an object that represents the page and then pass the Selenium object in the programming language. So let us now create our first Page Object against the home page.

1. Create a new Java class in IDEA called HomePage.
2. Import the relevant packages for the tests to run.

3. We will now need a constructor to handle Selenium. You may want to make it go to the home page when it is instantiated too. An example of this can be seen as follows:

HomePage.java

```java
import org.openqa.selenium.By;
import org.openqa.selenium.WebDriver;

public class HomePage{
  WebDriver selenium;
  public HomePage(WebDriver selenium){
    this.selenium = selenium;
  }
  public Chapter2 clickChapter2(){
    clickChapter("2");
    return new Chapter2(selenium);
  }

  private void clickChapter(String number){
    selenium.findElement(By.linkText("Chapter"+number)).click();
  }
}
```

Chapter2.java

```java
import org.openqa.selenium.By;
import org.openqa.selenium.WebDriver;

public class Chapter2 {
  WebDriver selenium;
  public Chapter2(WebDriver selenium){
    this.selenium = selenium;
    if (!"Chapter 2".equalsIgnoreCase(
      this.selenium.getTitle())){
        selenium.get(
          "http://book.theautomatedtester.co.uk/chapter2");
      }
  }
  public boolean isButtonPresent(String button){
    return selenium.findElements(By.xpath("//input[@id='" +
      button + "']")).size()>0;
  }
}
```

BestPractises3.java

```java
import org.junit.After;
import org.junit.Before;
```

```java
import org.junit.Test;
import org.openqa.selenium.WebDriver;
import org.openqa.selenium.firefox.FirefoxDriver;

public class BestPractises3 {
  WebDriver selenium;

  @Before
  public void setUp(){
    selenium = new FirefoxDriver();
  }

  @After
  public void tearDown(){
    selenium.quit();
  }

  @Test
  public void
    ShouldLoadTheHomePageAndThenCheckButtonOnChapter2(){
    selenium.get("http://book.theautomatedtester.co.uk");
    HomePage hp = new HomePage(selenium);
    Chapter2 ch2 = hp.clickChapter2();
    assertTrue(ch2.isButtonPresent("but1"));
  }
}
```

4. If you create these three files you will see it pass. The test is a lot more succinct and easier to maintain.

What just happened?

In this section we had a look at creating tests using the Page Object design pattern. This allows us to create objects in a programming language and then pass the Selenium object to it to drive the browser. This creates a really nice DSL that allows all parties in the development cycle to understand. We create a Java object for each of the pages that we want to work against on the site. We then just instantiate the class to work against that page.

When we are moving between pages you click on a link and the method controlling the page transition will return an object representing a new page.

The objects will not hold the asserts; this should always be done within the tests.

Pop quiz – Page Object design pattern

1. What is the Page Object design pattern?

Using Page Factories with Page Objects

The code that we have learnt to write earlier can be quite verbose. To clean up our code, we can start to use Page Factories. This allows us to annotate variables in our page objects with how to search the page. This means that we don't have to have full `WebElement element = driver.findElement(...);` code all over the file. We can change it to:

```
@FindBy(how=How.ID, using="foo")
WebElement foo;
```

As you can see this can make our code slightly easier to read and therefore more maintainable. If you regularly use other languages like Ruby or Python, you will notice that they don't have the PageFactory support project. This is because those languages don't have `Factory` constructs in the language. They are not idiomatic and therefore not in the language.

To use the PageFactory project in WebDriver, we will have to make sure that the we have added it as a dependency.

Let us now update our previous code from with an example of the PageFactory.

Time for action – using PageFactory

In this example we are going to be cleaning up the previous examples by using the PageFactory. This will allow us to create more succinct code than the previous verbose examples.

1. Open the previous example and go to `Chapter2.java`. It should look like the following example:

Chapter2.java

```
import org.openqa.selenium;
import junit.framework.Assert;

public class Chapter2 {
  WebDriver selenium;
  WebElement verifybutton;

  public Chapter2(WebDriver selenium){
    this.selenium = selenium;
    verifybutton = selenium.findElement(By.id("verifybutton"));
    if (!"Chapter 2".equalsIgnoreCase(
```

```
            this.selenium.getTitle())){
            selenium.get(
                "http://book.theautomatedtester.co.uk/chapter2");
        }
    }

    public boolean isButtonPresent(String button){
        return selenium.findElements(By.xpath
            ("//input[@id='"+button+"']")).size()>0;
    }

}
```

2. We can then change the line that looks for `verifybutton` so that it is not in the constructor. This then changes to:

```
public class Chapter2 {
    WebDriver selenium;

    @FindBy(how= How.NAME, using="verifybutton")
    WebElement verifybutton;

    public Chapter2(WebDriver selenium){
        this.selenium = selenium;
        if (!"Chapter 2".equalsIgnoreCase(
            this.selenium.getTitle())){
            selenium.get(
                "http://book.theautomatedtester.co.uk/chapter2");
        }
    }

    public bool isButton(String button){
        return selenium.findElementByXpath(
            '//button[@id='+button+']');
    }

}
```

3. If you run your test now, you will see it do the same thing but we have not called the `findElement()` method available to WebDriver.

4. In the test we need to initialize the factory by calling `initElements()`:

TestChapter2.java

```java
import org.openqa.selenium.*;
import org.junit.*;

public class TestChapter2 {
  WebDriver selenium;

  @Before
  public void setUp(){
    selenium = new FirefoxDriver();
  }

  @After
  public void tearDown(){
    selenium.quit();
  }

  public Chapter2 clickChapter2(){
    clickChapter("2");
    return  PageFactory.initElements(selenium, Chapter2.class);
  }
  @Test
  public void ShouldLoadTheHomePageAndThenCheckButtonOnChapter2() {
    selenium.get("http://book.theautomatedtester.co.uk");
    HomePage hp = new HomePage(selenium);
    Chapter2 ch2 = hp.clickChapter2();
    assertTrue(ch2.isButtonPresent("but1"));
  }

}
```

What just happened?

We have just seen how we can get rid of a line of code from a constructor or a method by adding a decorator to the variable. When our code is compiled, the variable will get populated at the right time so that we can make sure that it gets the right bit of the DOM. It will look like our element hasn't been instantiated. When we initialize the PageFactory, by calling `initElements()` it will populate the variables with the right data.

This does make a lot of the code a lot more succinct and can be a lot easier to maintain over time.

One thing to note is that every time we use the element it will be searched. We can get Selenium WebDriver to cache the return of the results by adding another decorator:

```
@FindBy(how=How.ID, using="verifybutton")
@CacheLookup
WebElement verifybutton;
```

 We only want to cache the result on a fairly static page. If you have a site that has a lot of JavaScript, you will not want to put @CacheLookup as you may start getting StaleElementException when you try to use it.

Pop quiz – Page Factories

1. What is the decorator that you put above a webelement variable when looking for an element by ID with the id='myId'?
2. How do you cache the lookup of web elements?
3. How do you initialize a Page Factory?

LoadableComponent

LoadableComponent is another way to approach PageObjects. LoadableComponent is a base class that all of the pages need to extend. The base class has the following methods on the interface:

- get()
- isLoaded()
- load()

Instead of the usual public class PageObject, we change it:

```
public class PageObject extends LoadableComponent<PageObject>
```

We will have to add overrides for the load() and isLoaded() method. The load method will load the page for us and the isLoaded() method can allow us to check if the page has been loaded correctly.

For example:

```
@override
Protected void load() {
  selenium.get("http://book.theautomatedtester.co.uk");
}

@protected void isLoaded() {
  String url = selenium.getCurrentUrl();
  If (url != "http://book.theautomatedtester.co.uk"){
    throw new Exception("The wrong page has loaded");
  }
}
```

As we can see this is just a simple bit of code, but we can make sure that we start on the right page when we need to.

Time for action – changing our Page Object to use LoadableComponent

Now that we have learnt about LoadableComponents, we should have a look at seeing it in action. We need to make changes to our Java Class.

1. The following is how the code should look so far:

```
public class Chapter2 {
  WebDriver selenium;

  @FindBy(how= How.NAME, using="verifybutton")
  WebElement verifybutton;

  public Chapter2(WebDriver selenium){
    this.selenium = selenium;
    if (!"Chapter 2".equalsIgnoreCase(this.selenium.getTitle())){
      selenium.get("http://book.theautomatedtester.co.uk/
        chapter2");
    }
  }

  public boolean isButtonPresent(String button){
    return selenium.findElements(By.xpath
    ("//input[@id='"+button+"']")).size()>0;
  }
}
```

2. If we have a look at our Chapter 2 Java class, we can see that we need to extend LoadableComponent. Since this takes generics we will have to pass in our PageObject class. It should look like:

```
public class Chapter2 extends LoadableComponent<Chapter2> {
```

3. In our constructor, we will have to initialize our page factory. We can remove the rest of the code in there since that will be moved to `load()`. It should look like the following:

```
public Chapter2(WebDriver selenium){
    this.selenium = selenium;
    PageFactory.initElements(selenium, this);
}
```

4. We now need to add our override methods. These will allow us to check that we are on the right page when we load this component:

```
@override
Protected void load() {
    selenium.get("http://book.theautomatedtester.co.uk/chapter2");
}

@protected void isLoaded() {
    String url = selenium.getCurrentUrl();
    If (url != "http://book.theautomatedtester.co.uk/chapter2"){
        throw new Exception("The wrong page has loaded");
    }
}
```

5. Now we need to have a look at updating our test to load everything for us. To do this we need to change:

```
@Test
public void ShouldLoadTheHomePageAndThenCheckButtonOnChapter2() {
    selenium.get("http://book.theautomatedtester.co.uk");
    HomePage hp = new HomePage(selenium);
    Chapter2 ch2 = hp.clickChapter2();
    assertTrue(ch2.isButtonPresent("but1"));
    }
```

6. To look like this:

```
@Test
public void ShouldLoadTheHomePageAndThenCheckButtonOnChapter2(){
    Chapter2 cht = new Chapter2(selenium).get();

    ch2.isButton("but1");
}
```

7. Run your test. Everything should look like the following:

```
public class Chapter2 extends LoadableComponent<Chapter2>{
  WebDriver selenium;

  @FindBy(how= How.NAME, using="verifybutton")
  WebElement verifybutton;

  public Chapter2(WebDriver selenium){
    this.selenium = selenium;
    PageFactory.initElements(selenium, this);
  }

  @override
  Protected void load() {
    selenium.get("http://book.theautomatedtester.co.uk/chapter2");
  }

  @protected
  public void isLoaded() {
    String url = selenium.getCurrentUrl();
    If (url != "http://book.theautomatedtester.co.uk/chapter2"){
      throw new Exception("The wrong page has loaded");
    }
  }

  public boolean isButtonDisplayed(String button){
    return selenium.findElement(By.id("button")).isDisplayed();
  }
}
```

What just happened?

We have just converted our page object to use the LoadableComponent class that comes with the Selenium Project. We saw how we simplified on constructors and then just moved this into somewhere easy to maintain. We have seen that we can move a lot of the boiler plate code out of our class and rely on it being pulled in via LoadableComponent. This means that we no longer need to maintain it or we add those items.

Have a go hero – LoadableComponent

Imagine how you have to work with a flow that takes you through a number of pages. LoadableComponent allows us to set up a workflow. To get this right we need to pass one in like the following when doing your test setup:

```
@Before
public void prepareComponents() {
    WebDriver selenium = new FirefoxDriver();

    HomePage homePage = new HomePage(selenium);
    Chapter2 chapter2 = new SecuredPage(selenium, homePage);

}
```

Summary

We learnt a lot in this chapter about design patterns that we can use with Selenium WebDriver. We have learnt techniques that allow us to build test projects that are easy to maintain and readable by all users.

Specifically, we covered:

♦ **Page Objects**: This is a technique where we split the test logic out into separate classes. This allows us to create a Java class for each of the pages that we use on the page.

♦ **Page Factory**: This allows us to decorate our WebElement variables in our Page objects so that we remove a lot of the look up code. We learnt that the elements get initialized when we call `PageFactory.initElements();` in our tests or anything else that may use that code.

♦ **LoadableComponent**: In this section we had a look at the base page for Page Objects that comes with the Selenium Project. The LoadableComponent in a base class allows us to remove quite a bit of code and moves the boilerplate to LoadableComponent.

Now that we've learnt about design patterns, we're ready to look at the last advanced techniques that we can use with Selenium WebDriver—which is the topic of the next chapter.

5

Finding Elements

In this chapter we are going to be looking at how we go about finding elements on the page using the WebDriver API. One of the things that we learnt in the previous chapter was that WebDriver, due to its architecture, has two major components. The first one is the "driver". This has the commands to find the elements.

We will start by having a look at the different commands. We begin with the helper commands first and then go to the more generic commands which take different types of objects. We will finish off the chapter by learning some helpful techniques when interacting with element finding.

First major learning point:

◆ Finding element(s) on the page by their ID, name, ClassName, XPath, and link list

◆ Tips for using find element calls

So let's get on with it...

Important preliminary points

When working through the following examples we are going to assume that you have instantiated a WebDriver object by doing:

```
WebDriver driver = new FirefoxDriver();
```

You can use the following example class with JUnit 4. The test is a stub that we can use through the chapter.

```
import org.junit.*;
import org.openqa.selenium.*;
import org.openqa.selenium.firefox.*;

import java.io.File;
import java.util.Dictionary;

public class TestExample1 {

  Webdriver driver;

  @Before
  public void setUp(){
    driver = new FirefoxDriver();
    driver.get("http://book.theautomatedtester.co.uk/chapter1");
  }

  @After
  public void tearDown(){
    driver.quit();
  }

  @Test
  public void testExamples(){
    // We will put examples in here
  }
```

We should also note that finding elements can also be achieved from an element. For example, if we wanted to find the first link after a button called button we would do something like the following:

```
WebElement element = ((FindsById)driver).findElementById("button");
WebElement childElement = element.findElement(By.tagName("a"));
```

We will go into what this means in depth as we go through the chapter.

Finding elements

When working with WebDriver on a web application, we will need to find elements on the page. This is the core to being able to work. All the methods for doing actions to the web application like typing and clicking require that we find the element first.

Finding an element on the page by its ID

The first item that we are going to look at is finding an element by ID. Finding elements by ID will be one of the easiest ways to find an element. We are going to start with `findElementByID()`. This method is a helper method that sets an argument for a more generic `findElement` call. We will see now how we can use it in action. The method's signature looks like:

```
findElementById(String using);
```

The `using` variable takes the ID of the element that you wish to look for. It will return a `WebElement` object that we can then work with.

Time for action – using findElementById()

We are going to find an element on the page by using the `findElementById()` method that is on each of the Browser Driver classes. `findElement` calls will return a `WebElement` object that we can perform actions on.

Follow these steps to see how it works:

1. Open your Java IDE. Intellij or Eclipse are the most used.

2. We are going to use the command:

    ```
    WebElement element = ((FindsById)driver).
        findElementById("verifybutton");
    ```

3. Run the test from the IDE. It will look like the following screenshot:

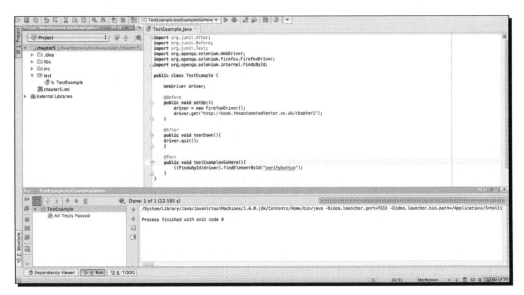

What just happened?

We have just seen how we can find an element by using the `findElementById` helper method. After running the test, we saw that it passed. This meant that it found the element. If an element is not found in Selenium, WebDriver will throw a `NoSuchElementFoundException` exception.

Finding elements on the page by their ID

In addition to `findElementById`, there is `findElementsByID`. This call has been added to the API so that there is symmetry in the API even though it is against the HTML spec to have more than one item in the DOM with an ID. We will now see how we can use it in action. The method's signature looks like:

```
findElementsById(String using);
```

The using variable takes the ID of the element that you wish to look for. It will return a `WebElement` object that we can then work with.

Time for action – using findElementsById()

We are going to find an element on the page by using the `findElementsById()` method that is on each of the Browser Driver classes. `findElement` calls will return a `WebElement` object that we can do actions on.

Follow these steps to see how it works:

1. Open your Java IDE. Intellij or Eclipse are the most used.

2. We are going to use the command:

    ```
    List<WebElement> elements = ((FindsById)driver)
      .findElementsById("verifybutton");
    Assert.equals(1, elements.size());
    ```

3. Run the test from the IDE. It will look like the following screenshot:

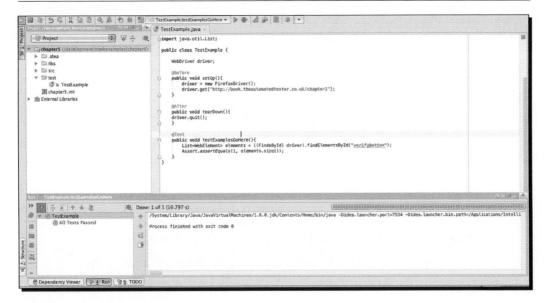

What just happened?

We have just seen how we can find an element by using the `findElementsById` helper method. After running the test, we saw that it passed. Unlike its singular version, it will not throw a `NoSuchElementException` exception if the element is not found. It will return a list that has a size of zero.

Finding an element on the page by its name

The next item that we are going to look at is finding an element by their name. Finding elements by name is just as fast as their ID equivalent. This method is a helper method that sets an argument for a more generic `findElement` call. We will now see how we can use it in action. The method's signature looks like:

```
findElementByName(String using);
```

The using variable takes the ID of the element that you wish to look for. It will return a `WebElement` object that we can then work with.

Time for action – using findElementByName()

We are going to find an element on the page by using the `findElementByName()` method that is on each of the Browser Driver classes. `findElement` calls will return a `WebElement` object that we can perform actions on.

Follow these steps to see how it works:

1. Open your Java IDE. Intellij or Eclipse are the most used.

2. We are going to use the command:

```
WebElement element = ((FindsByName)driver).
   findElementByName("selected(1234)");
```

3. Run the test from the IDE. It will look like the following screenshot:

What just happened?

We have just seen how we can find an element by using the `findElementByName` helper method. After running the test, we saw that it passed. This meant that it found the element. If an element is not found in Selenium, WebDriver will throw a `NotSuchElementFound` exception.

Finding elements on the page by their name

Unlike ID, we can have multiple elements on the page that have the same name. This is also a symmetrical call to find multiple elements. We will now see how we can use it in action. The method's signature looks like:

```
findElementsByName(String using);
```

The using variable takes the ID of the element that you wish to look for. It will return a `WebElement` object that we can then work with.

Time for action – using findElementsByName()

We are going to find an element on the page by using the `findElementsByName()` method that is on each of the Browser Driver classes. `findElement` calls will return a list of `WebElement` objects that we can perform actions on.

Follow these steps to see how it works:

1. Open your Java IDE. Intellij or Eclipse are the most used.

2. We are going to use the command:

```
List<WebElement> elements = ((FindsByName)driver).
   findElementByName("selected(1234)");
Assert.equals(1, elements.size());
```

3. Run the test from the IDE. It will look like the following screenshot:

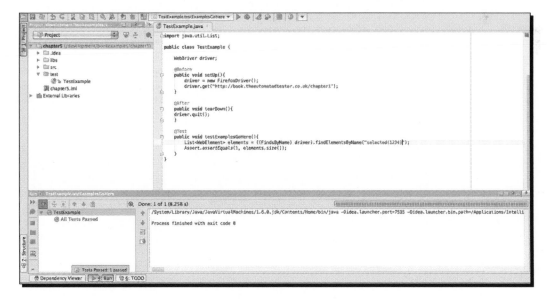

What just happened?

We have just seen how we can find an element by using the findElementsByName helper method. After running the test, we saw that it passed. Unlike its singular version, it will not throw a NoSuchElementException if the element is not found. It will return a list that has a size of zero.

Finding an element on the page by their ClassName

We are going to now look at findElementByClassName(). If there is more than one element on the page that has this class name, then it will return the first element that it gets.

We will now see how we can use it in action. The method's signature looks like the following:

```
findElementByClassName(String using);
```

The using variable takes the ID of the element that you wish to look for. It will return a WebElement object that we can then work with.

Time for action – using findElementByClassName()

We are going to find an element on the page by using findElementByClassName() method that is on each of the Browser Driver classes. findElement calls will return a WebElement object that we can do actions on.

Follow these steps to see how it works:

1. Open your Java IDE. Intellij or Eclipse are the most used.

2. We are going to use the command:

```
WebElement element = ((FindsByClassName)driver).
    findElementByClassName("storetext");
```

3. Run the test from the IDE. It will look like the following screenshot:

What just happened?

We have just seen how we can find an element by using the `findElementByClassName` helper method. After running the test, we saw that it passed. This meant that it found the element. If an element is not found in Selenium, WebDriver will throw a `NotSuchElementFound` exception.

Finding elements on the page by their ClassName

We will now see how we can use it in action. The method's signature looks like:

```
findElementsByClass(String using);
```

The using variable takes the ID of the element that you wish to look for. It will return a `WebElement` object that we can then work with.

Time for action – using findElementsByClassName()

We are going to find an element on the page by using `findElementByClassName()` method that is on each of the Browser Driver classes. `findElement` calls will return a `WebElement` object that we can do actions on.

Follow these steps to see it work:

1. Open your Java IDE. Intellij or Eclipse are the most used that you could use.

2. We are going to use the command:

```
List<WebElement> elements = ((FindsByClassName)driver)
  .findElementsByClassName("storetext");
Assert.equals(1, elements.size());
```

3. Run the test from the IDE. It will look like the following screenshot:

What just happened?

We have just seen how we can find an element by using the `findElementsByClassName` helper method. After running the test, we saw that it passed. Unlike its singular version, it will not throw a `NoSuchElementException` if the element is not found. It will return a list that has a size of zero. If you want to use CSS selectors, you can use `findElementByCssSelector` or `findElementsByCssSelector`. In the next section, we will have a look at XPaths.

Finding an element on the page by their XPath

XPath is one of the most useful approaches to finding elements on the page. It has a bit of a tainted past due to the speed that it takes to look up elements on the page. We learnt a number of different techniques using XPath earlier in the book.

This method is a helper method that sets an argument for a more generic `findElement` call. We will now see how we can use it in action. The method's signature looks like the following:

```
findElementByXpath(String using);
```

The using variable takes the ID of the element that you wish to look for. It will return a `WebElement` object that we can then work with.

Time for action – using findElementByXPath()

We are going to find an element on the page by using the `findElementByXPath()` method that is on each of the Browser Driver classes. `findElement` calls will return a `WebElement` object that we can perform actions on.

Follow these steps to see it work:

1. Open your Java IDE. Intellij or Eclipse are the most used.

2. We are going to use the command:

```
WebElement element = ((FindsByXPath)driver).
   findElementByXpath("verifybutton");
```

3. Run the test from the IDE. It will look like the following screenshot:

What just happened?

We have just seen how we can find an element by using the `findElementByXPath` helper method. After running the test, we saw that it passed meaning that the XPath that we passed in works. If an element is not found in Selenium, WebDriver will throw a `NotSuchElementFound` exception.

Finding elements on the page by their XPath

We will now see how we can use it in action. The method's signature looks like:

```
findElementsByXpath(String using);
```

The `using` variable takes the ID of the element that you wish to look for. It will return a `WebElement` object that we can then work with.

Time for action – using findElementsByXpath()

We are going to find an element on the page by using the `findElementsByXPath()` method that is on each of the Browser Driver classes. `findElement` calls will return a `WebElement` object that we can perform actions on.

Follow these steps to see it work:

1. Open your Java IDE. Intellij or Eclipse are the most used.

2. We are going to use the command:

```
List<WebElement> elements = ((FindsByXPath)driver).
   findElementsByXpath("//input");
Assert.equals(5, elements.size());
```

3. Run the test from the IDE. It will look like the following screenshot:

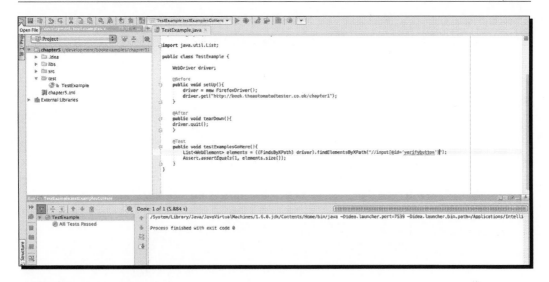

What just happened?

We have just seen how we can find an element by using the `findElementsByXPath` helper method. We saw that from running the test we saw it pass. Unlike its singular version, it will not throw a `NoSuchElement` exception if the element is not found. It will return a list that has a size of zero.

Finding an element on the page by its link text

If you need to find a link by the text that is in it, this method is useful. It is a helper method that sets an argument for a more generic `findElement` call. We will now see how we can use it in action. The method's signature looks like:

```
findElementByLinkText(String using);
```

The using variable takes the link text of the element that you wish to look for. It will return a `WebElement` object that we can then work with.

Time for action – using findElementByLinkText()

We are going to find an element on the page by using the `findElementByLinkText()` method that is on each of the Browser Driver classes. `findElement` calls will return a `WebElement` object that we can perform actions on.

Follow these steps to see it work:

1. Open your Java IDE. Intellij or Eclipse are the most used.

2. We are going to use the following command. We will use a different page on the site for this example.

```
Driver.get("http://book.theautomatedtester.co.uk")
WebElement element = ((FindsByLinkText)driver).
  findElementByLinkText("Chapter1");
```

3. Run the test from the IDE. It will look like the following screenshot:

What just happened?

We have just seen how we can find an element by using the `findElementByLinkText` helper method. One thing to note is that the search for the text is case sensitive when used in WebDriver. This means that what we pass into Selenium, WebDriver needs to match exactly or it will not find your element. If an element is not found in Selenium, WebDriver will throw a `NoSuchElementFound` exception.

Finding elements on the page by their link text

We will now see how we can find elements on the page by their link text in action. The method's signature looks like:

```
findElementsByLinkText(String using);
```

The using variable takes the link text of the element that you wish to look for. It will return a `WebElement` object that we can then work with.

Time for action – using findElementsByLinkText()

We are going to find an element on the page by using the `findElementsByLinkText()` method that is on each of the Browser Driver classes. `findElements` calls will return a list of `WebElement` objects that we can perform actions on.

Follow these steps to see it work:

1. Open your Java IDE. Intellij or Eclipse are the most used.

2. We are going to use the command.

   ```
   driver.get("http://book.theautomatedtester.co.uk")
   List<WebElement> elements = ((FindsByLinkText)driver).
     findElementsByLinkText("Chapter1");
   Assert.equals(1, elements.size());
   ```

3. Run the test from the IDE. It will look like the following screenshot:

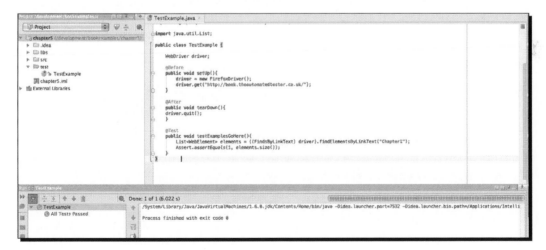

What just happened?

We have just seen how we can find an element by using the `findElementsByLinkText` helper method. One thing to note is that the search for the text is case sensitive. If an element is not found in Selenium, WebDriver will return an empty list.

Pop quiz – finding elements using helper methods

1. What is the best call for finding multiple elements using XPath?

   a. `findElementByXpath`

   b. `findElementsByXPath`

   c. `findElementByCssSelector`

2. What is the best call to an element using CSS selectors to find an element just on the class name?

   a. `findElementById`

   b. `findElementsByCssSelector`

   c. `findElementByClassName`

3. Will a `findElements` type call throw a `NoSuchElementException` when it can't find the element?

Have a go hero – using findElement Helper methods

Try creating an example where you need to find an element by CSS selector. This is used by `findElementByCssSelector` and `findElementsByCssSelector`. Have a try!

Finding elements using a more generic method

We have had a look at using helper methods to find elements on the page. The downside to using them is that if something changes, you need to change the entire method that you are using to find the element. This can increase the maintenance costs for doing this.

The other approach is to use the `findElement()` method, pass in the `By` abstract class, and call static methods on that class.

Let's see this in action.

Time for action – using findElement()

In this section we are going to look at using the `findElement` call that is on the WebDriver object. This is how we can normally find elements using Selenium WebDriver.

1. Open your Java IDE. Intellij or Eclipse are the most used that you could use.

2. We are going to use the command:

    ```
    driver.get("http://book.theautomatedtester.co.uk")
    driver.findElement(By.linkText("Chapter1"));
    ```

3. Run your test.

What just happened?

We have just seen that we can find an element by passing in the `By` object. This is a static class that gives people a mechanism for finding elements, as we did earlier in the chapter. This will throw a `NoSuchElementException` if it cannot find the element.

Let's now have a look at finding multiple elements.

Time for action – using findElements()

In this section we are going to look at using the `findElements` call that is on the WebDriver object. This is how we can normally find elements using Selenium WebDriver.

1. Open your Java IDE. Intellij or Eclipse are the most used.

2. We are going to use the command:

    ```
    driver.get("http://book.theautomatedtester.co.uk")
    List<WebElement> elements = driver.findElements(
        By.linkText("Chapter1"));
    Assert.assertEqual(1, elements.size());
    ```

3. Run your test.

What just happened?

We have used this similar to calls earlier in the chapter. This will find multiple elements on the page and return a list. This will not throw a `NoSuchElement` exception if it cannot find the element.

Tips and tricks

In this section, we are going to look at some tips and tricks that might be of use when trying to find elements on the page. We can also apply them to see if the elements are not on the page.

Finding if an element exists without throwing an error

Selenium WebDriver is really good at letting you know when an element does not exist. If it throws a NoSuchElementException, then we know it's not there. Unfortunately I, and many others, have not been big fans of using exception handling as a way of flow control.

To get around this we can use the findElements() call, and then we just need to check that the size of the list returned is 0. For example:

```
List<WebElement> elements = driver.findElements(
  By.Id("myElement"));
elements.size(); //This should be zero and can be checked accordingly
```

Waiting for elements to appear on the page

Web applications now want to appear as though they are desktop applications as more and more people move to hardware like tablets or netbooks which have very small hard drives. This is all done through AJAX to the page.

This means that when we are working with Selenium WebDriver we need to have it synchronized with what is happening on the page. We do not want to use something like Thread.sleep() because that doesn't make our tests run as quickly as possible. We need to use one of the next two approaches: implicit or explicit waits.

Implicit waits

Selenium WebDriver has borrowed the idea of implicit waits from Watir. This means that we can tell Selenium that we would like it to wait for a certain amount of time before throwing an exception that it cannot find the element on the page. We should note that implicit waits will be in place for the entire time the browser is open. This means that any search for elements on the page could take the time the implicit wait is set for.

Let's see how we can use this.

Time for action – using implicit waits

In this section we will see how we can use implicit waits in our code. We need to change a number of calls together to set the implicit. This was done to keep the API as succinct as possible:

1. Open your Java IDE. Intellij or Eclipse are the most used.

2. We are going to use the command:
   ```
   driver.manage().timeouts().implicitlyWait(10, TimeUnit.SECONDS);
   driver.findElement(By.xpath("//div[@id='ajaxdiv']")
   ```

3. Run your tests:

```
25        @Test
26   ⊟    public void testExamples(){
27            driver.manage().timeouts().implicitlyWait(10, TimeUnit.SECONDS);
28            driver.findElement(By.xpath("//div[@id='ajaxdiv']"));
29   ⊟    }
30   ⊟  }
31
```

```
one: 1 of 1 (32.066 s)

   /System/Library/Java/JavaVirtualMachines/1.6.0.jdk/Contents/Home/bin/java -Didea.launcher.port=7535 "-[

   Process finished with exit code 0
```

What just happened?

We have just seen that our tests run and pass. We didn't have to do anything special for waiting for the new text to appear on the page. Let's go see how we can do this with the explicit waiting approach.

Explicit waits

Unfortunately implicit waits do not fit all situations and for some developers is not the right thing to do. Explicit waits is when we know what we want to happen and the error needs to fit that situation.

Let's see this in action!

Time for action – using explicit waits with Selenium WebDriver

In this section we will have a look at using explicit waits. This is useful for making sure that the right type of exception is thrown:

1. Open your Java IDE.

2. We are going to use the following code. `WebDriverWait` is found in the Support package within the Selenium WebDriver Jar.

```
WebElement element = (new WebDriverWait(driver, 10))
  .until(new ExpectedCondition<WebElement>(){
    @Override
    public WebElement apply(WebDriver d) {
      return d.findElement(By.xpath("//div[@id='ajaxdiv']")
}});
```

3. Run your tests:

```
26      @Test
27      public void testExamples(){
28          WebElement element = (new WebDriverWait(driver, 10))
29                  .until(new ExpectedCondition<WebElement>(){
30                      @Override
31                      public WebElement apply(WebDriver d) {
32                          return d.findElement(By.xpath("//div[@id='ajaxdiv']"));
33                      }});
34
35      }
36  }
```

Done: 1 of 1 (29.637 s)

```
/System/Library/Java/JavaVirtualMachines/1.6.0.jdk/Contents/Home/bin/java –Didea.launch
Process finished with exit code 0
```

What just happened?

We have just seen how we can use an explicit wait with our code. We told the wait class that we wanted it to wait ten seconds while trying to find the element. I personally prefer explicit waits since you can see by reading the code how long it is going to wait for.

Let's now see what we have learnt in this chapter.

Summary

We learnt a lot in this chapter about finding elements using the Selenium WebDriver Element.

Specifically, we covered:

- **Finding elements with helper methods**: We saw what is needed to get things running and finding elements on the page using Selenium WebDriver. We started with the helper methods so that we can just start finding elements. In the next section we saw how we can make them more robust.

- **Finding elements in a maintainable way**: In this section we learnt how to find elements in a more maintainable approach. We just need to change the argument in the method signature.

- **Tips and tricks**: Here we learnt how we can find an element without throwing an exception. We also had a look at waiting for elements to appear on the page. Elements can happen asynchronously so we never know when they will appear.

Now that we've learnt about finding elements, we're ready to start using browsers and tweaking them to our needs—which is the topic of the next chapter.

6

Working with WebDriver

In the last chapter we saw how we can look for elements. Now let's start working with Selenium WebDriver in different browsers. Remember that Selenium WebDriver is a browser automation framework for all of the major browsers and can access the browser like an end user would.

In this chapter, we shall:

- ◆ Run a test with Firefox
    - ❑ Working with Firefox profiles

- ◆ Run a test with Google Chrome or Chromium
    - ❑ Updating the capabilities of the browser

- ◆ Run a test with Opera
    - ❑ Working with Opera Profiles

- ◆ Run a test with Internet Explorer
    - ❑ Working with InternetExplorerDriver

So let's get on with it...

Important preliminary points

You will need to download the following items. Make sure that you download the relevant executable for your environment:

- IE Driver Executable: `http://code.google.com/p/selenium/downloads/list`
- Chrome Driver Executable: `http://code.google.com/p/chromium/downloads/list`
- Opera Driver Executable: `https://github.com/operasoftware/operadriver/downloads`
- Firefox Driver does not require a download as it is bundled with the Java client bindings

Please make sure that you have all the necessary browsers installed to complete all the sections of this chapter.

When working through the following examples, we are going to assume that you have instantiated a WebDriver object by doing:

```
WebDriver driver = new FirefoxDriver();
```

You can use the following example class for use with JUnit 4:

```
import org.junit.*;
import org.openqa.selenium.*;
import org.openqa.selenium.firefox.*;

import java.io.File;
import java.util.Dictionary;

public class TestChapter6 {

  WebDriver driver;

  @Before
  public void setUp(){
    driver = //we will update this part with each section
    driver.get("http://book.theautomatedtester.co.uk/chapter4");
    }

  @After
  public void tearDown(){
    driver.quit();
    }
```

```
@Test
public void testExamples(){
  // We will put examples in here
  }
}
```

Working with FirefoxDriver

FirefoxDriver is the easiest driver to use, since everything that we need to use is all bundled with the Java client bindings that we used in the previous chapter.

In the next section we are going to see about loading the browser and typing to the screen. This is what we will be doing in most of our applications.

Time for action – loading the FirefoxDriver

We are going to do the basic task of loading the browser and type into the page.

1. Update the setUp() method to load the FirefoxDriver();

   ```
   driver = new FirefoxDriver();
   ```

2. Now we need to find an element. In this section we will find the one with the ID nextBid:

   ```
   WebElement element = driver.findElement(By.id("nextBid"));
   ```

3. Now we need to type into that element:

   ```
   element.sendKeys("100");
   ```

4. Run your test and it should look like the following:

   ```
   public class TestChapter6 {

     WebDriver driver;

     @Before
     public void setUp(){
       driver = new FirefoxDriver();
       driver.get("http://book.theautomatedtester.co.uk/chapter4");
     }

     @After
     public void tearDown(){
       driver.quit();
   ```

```
        }

    @Test
    public void testExamples(){
        WebElement element = driver.findElement(By.id("nextBid"));
        element.sendKeys("100");
    }
}
```

What just happened?

We have just seen how easy it is to run a test with Selenium WebDriver and Firefox. It loaded the browser and then typed into the browser. We can now do everything and anything that we want to the content that is loaded into the browser. Now let's have a look at all the other things that we can do with FirefoxDriver.

Firefox profile preferences

There are times where we need to update the preferences within Firefox. This could be to switch on parts of Firefox that are disabled while they are in development or if you want to get more information from the browser while your tests are running. To do this, we will need to instantiate a Firefox Profile object and then update the settings.

We will then need to pass this object into FirefoxDriver where we instantiate it. This will load the profile with your details you have set. This is like loading about:config in the browser and changing what you need to.

Let's see how we can do this with a code sample.

Time for action – setting Firefox preferences

Imagine that you wanted to have your site as the startup page for Firefox. To do this we will need to update the browser.startup.homepage preference. Follow these steps:

1. Let's start by creating the FirefoxProfile object:

```
FirefoxProfile profile = new FirefoxProfile();
```

2. Now we will set the preference:

```
profile.setPreference("browser.startup.homepage",
    "http://book,theautomatedtester.co.uk");
```

3. To get the profile to be used, we need to pass it in to the driver. To do this, we need to do the following:

```
driver = new FirefoxDriver(profile);
```

4. Run your test. The final code should look like the following:

```
public class TestChapter6 {

    WebDriver driver;

    @Before
    public void setUp(){
    FirefoxProfile profile = new FirefoxProfile();
    profile.setPreference("browser.startup.homepage",
       "http://book,theautomatedtester.co.uk/chapter4");
       driver = new FirefoxDriver(profile);
       }

    @After
    public void tearDown(){
       driver.quit();
    }

    @Test
    public void testExamples(){
       WebElement element = driver.findElement(By.id("nextBid"));
       element.sendKeys("100");
    }
}
```

What just happened?

We have just seen that we can manipulate Firefox settings before the browser is loaded. This can be useful if you need to get extra information out of the browser or if we have a few things that need tweaking.

If you had installed Firefox in a different place, you would have had to instantiate the FirefoxBinary class with details of it:

```
FirefoxBinary binary = new FirefoxBinary("/path/to/binary");
driver = new FirefoxDriver(binary);
```

If you need to update both the Firefox Profile and the Firefox Binary, you can simply pass both of them through the constructor as follows:

```
FirefoxBinary binary = new FirefoxBinary("/path/to/binary");
FirefoxProfile profile = new FirefoxProfile();
profile.setPreference("browser.startup.homepage",
  "http://book,theautomatedtester.co.uk/chapter4");

driver = new FirefoxDriver(binary, profile);
```

As you can see, it's fairly simple to load Firefox if it isn't installed in the usual place.

Installing a Firefox add-on

One of the most useful features of Firefox is the ability to install add-ons to enhance the user experience. This enhanced experience can mean that web applications act differently when the add-on is installed.

Let's have a look at how we can install an add-on into our profile before we start the browser.

Time for action – installing the add-on

Imagine that you wanted to install Firebug so that if a test were to fail we could try and debug the JavaScript. To do this, we will need to create a `FirefoxProfile` and then tell it to add the add-on.

1. Create a profile object:

```
FirefoxProfile profile = new FirefoxProfile();
```

2. Now we need to install the add-on. WebDriver can only install add-ons that are on the local hard drive:

```
profile.addExtension("path/to/addon");
```

3. Pass the profile into FirefoxDriver and then run your test. Your code would look like the following:

```
public class TestChapter6 {

    WebDriver driver;
```

```
@Before
public void setUp(){
    FirefoxProfile profile = new FirefoxProfile();
    profile.addExtension("firebug.xpi");
    driver = new FirefoxDriver(profile);
    driver.get("http://book.theautomatedtester.co.uk/chapter4");
}

@After
public void tearDown(){
    driver.quit();
}

@Test
public void testExamples(){
    WebElement element = driver.findElement(By.id("nextBid"));
    element.sendKeys("100");
}
}
```

What just happened?

We have just installed a Firefox add-on into the browser before we run our test. This is much simpler than it used to be in Selenium Remote Control where we would need to load the profile manually and make the changes that we needed and then run our tests telling Selenium Server to use this profile. The old process is not very portable compared to what we just did.

So far we have learnt to load Firefox and make changes to the browser before it loads which can be quite useful if we need to get more information out of the browser or make debugging issues a lot simpler. Let's see how much you remember with this quick pop quiz.

Pop quiz – working with FirefoxDriver

1. How would you set a preference?
2. How would you tell FirefoxDriver to use Firefox that is not installed in the usual place?

Have a go hero – installing Firebug and not loading the First Run page

A lot of people like to use Firebug with WebDriver but get really annoyed with the First Run page.

1. To get around this, we are going to have to update the version of Firebug in your Firefox Preferences.

2. We will set the version to 99.9:

```java
public class TestChapter6 {

    WebDriver driver;

    @Before
    public void setUp(){
        FirefoxProfile profile = new FirefoxProfile();
        profile.addExtension("firebug.xpi");
        profile.setPreference("extensions.firebug.currentVersion",
            "99.9");
        driver = new FirefoxDriver(profile);
        driver.get("http://book.theautomatedtester.co.uk/chapter4");
    }

    @After
    public void tearDown(){
        driver.quit();
    }

    @Test
    public void testExamples(){
        WebElement element = driver.findElement(By.id("nextBid"));
        element.sendKeys("100");
    }
}
```

Working with ChromeDriver

In this section, we will have a look at how we can start working with Google Chrome or with Chromium. Google Chrome or Chromium is in the top three browsers used in the world so most people want to make sure that their web applications work with it.

If you haven't downloaded the ChromeDriver you will need to do it now for the following sections. You will also need to set an environment path of where it is, so ChromeDriver in Java will know where to get it. This is purely for the ChromeDriver. If you have Google Chrome or Chromium installed somewhere that isn't the default, we will see how to handle that with ChromeOptions.

On Linux and Mac OS X do: `export PATH=$PATH:/path/to/chromedriver`.

On Windows do: `set PATH=$PATH;\path\to\chromedriver`.

Time for action – starting Google Chrome or Chromium

Imagine that you wanted to work with Google Chrome to get an attribute of an element on the page. To do this we will need to instantiate a ChromeDriver. Let's see an example.

1. Update the `setUp()` method to load the `ChromeDriver()`:

```
driver = new ChromeDriver();
```

2. Now we need to find an element. In this section we will find the one with the ID `selectLoad`:

```
WebElement element = driver.findElement(By.id("selectLoad"));
```

3. Now we need to get the value attribute of that element:

```
element.getAttribute("value");
```

4. Run your test and it should look like the following:

```
public class TestChapter6 {

    WebDriver driver;

    @Before
    public void setUp(){
        driver = new ChromeDriver();
        driver.get("http://book.theautomatedtester.co.uk/chapter4");
    }

    @After
    public void tearDown(){
        driver.quit();
    }

    @Test
    public void testExamples(){
```

```
    WebElement element = driver.findElement(
      By.id("selectLoad"));
    String value = element.getAttribute("value");
    Assert.assertEquals("Click to load the select below",
      value);
  }
}
```

What just happened?

We have just run a test with Google Chrome or with Chromium. It was fairly simple to get going and then the browser was able to get the value of the button. If you had trouble getting it to run, make sure that you have downloaded the ChromeDriver and added it to the environment variable called PATH.

Now that we have got ChromeDriver working, let's have a look at how we can update the browser as we did with Firefox.

ChromeOptions

Google Chrome or Chromium doesn't really have a profile that users can update in the same sense as Firefox. It does however have a mechanism that allows us to set certain options that Chrome will try and use. We can also tell it to install Chromium extensions, which are like Firefox add-ons, into the browser so we can enhance the experience.

Time for action – using ChromeOptions

Imagine that you needed to tell ChromeDriver the location of you Google Chrome or Chromium. To set this we will need to instantiate a ChromeOptions object and tell that where to find the Chrome/Chromium Binary.

Let's see how to do it:

1. Update the setUp() method to instantiate a ChromeOptions object and call setBinary() method:

   ```
   ChromeOptions options = new ChromeOptions();
   options.setBinary("/path/to/location");
   ```

2. Update the setUp() method to load the ChromeOptions object into the ChromeDriver:

   ```
   driver = new ChromeDriver(options);
   ```

3. Now we need to find an element. In this section we will find the one with the ID `selectLoad`:

```
WebElement element = driver.findElement(By.id("selectLoad"));
```

4. Now we need to get the value attribute of that element:

```
element.getAttribute("value");
```

5. Run your test and it should look like the following:

```
public class TestChapter6 {

    WebDriver driver;

    @Before
    public void setUp(){
      ChromeOptions options = new ChromeOptions();
      options.setBinary("/path/to/location");
      driver = new ChromeDriver(options);
      driver.get("http://book.theautomatedtester.co.uk/chapter4");
    }

    @After
    public void tearDown(){
      driver.quit();
    }

    @Test
    public void testExamples(){
      WebElement element = driver.findElement(
      By.id("selectLoad"));
      String value = element.getAttribute("value");
      Assert.assertEquals("Click to load the select below",
         value);
    }
}
```

What just happened?

We have just seen how we can inject options that we want Chrome or Chromium to start with. If we needed to pass in the arguments that we could start the browser with or if we needed to tell ChromeDriver, we can use `setArguments()`. This allows us to do many things to the browser. We can see a definitive list at `http://src.chromium.org/ viewvc/chrome/trunk/src/chrome/common/chrome_switches.cc?view=markup`.

If you have a Chrome Extension, a file with a `.crx` extension, you will need to use the `addExtension()` method as you would in FirefoxDriver. The following snippet will show an example:

```
ChromeOptions options = new ChromeOptions();
options.addExtension("example.crx")
```

Pop quiz – using ChromeDriver

1. What is the name of the object that allows us to tweak Chrome or Chromium before it launches?

2. What environment variable do we need to set and why?

Working with OperaDriver

Opera Software, the company that creates Opera, has created their own project to support Selenium WebDriver. Since not every web browser will act the same with the sites that we create, it is a good idea to make sure we can test our applications with OperaDriver.

Note that OperaDriver works best with the latest stable release of Opera. Make sure that you update regularly.

Let's see how easy OperaDriver is to use.

Time for action – starting Opera

In this section, we will see how we can start OperaDriver and get it to click a button on the page. This simple test will give us the confidence to use Selenium WebDriver with Opera.

1. Update the `setUp()` method to load the `OperaDriver()`:
   ```
   driver = new OperaDriver();
   ```

2. Now we need to find an element. In this section we will find the link Chapter 4:
   ```
   WebElement element = driver.findElement(By.linkText("Chapter 4"));
   ```

3. Now we need to click on the link:
   ```
   element.click();
   ```

4. Run your test and it should look like the following:

```java
public class TestChapter6 {

    WebDriver driver;

    @Before
    public void setUp(){
        driver = new OperaDriver();
        driver.get("http://book.theautomatedtester.co.uk/");

    }

    @After
    public void tearDown(){
        driver.quit();
    }

    @Test
    public void testExamples(){
        WebElement element = driver.findElement(
            By.linkText("Chapter 4"));
        element.click();

        // Assert that we only have 1 link
        Assert.assertEquals(1, driver.findElements(
            By.linkText("index")).size());
    }
}
```

What just happened?

We have just seen how easy it is to get the OperaDriver loading Opera and interacting with what is on the page. We used `click()` on a link so that we can navigate between pages. Just by changing the object that is instantiated in the `setUp()` method we got it to load.

Opera, like the previous browsers we have used, allows us to set details of the browser before the browser has started up. Let's have a look at how that works.

OperaProfile

The OperaProfile is a new addition to the OperaDriver. It allows us to set details in the browser when the browser starts. Opera Software tests the browser where it can, so we can set a lot of details of the browser. In the following example, we are going to disable Geolocation from our tests.

Time for action – working with OperaProfile

Imagine that you want to test your web application that uses geolocation in the browser, when it cannot use geolocation. All location-based applications need to support this if you were to get a user who is worried about privacy on certain machines.

1. Update the `setUp()` method to load the `OperaDriver()`:

```
OperaProfile profile = new OperaProfile();
profile.preferences().set("Geolocation",
  "Enable geolocation", false);
driver = new OperaDriver(profile);
```

2. Now we need to find an element. In this section we will find the link Chapter 4:

```
WebElement element = driver.findElement(By.linkTexxt(
  "Chapter 4"));
```

3. Now we need to click on the link:

```
element.click();
```

4. Run your test and it should look like the following:

```
public class TestChapter6 {

  WebDriver driver;

  @Before
  public void setUp(){
    OperaProfile profile = new OperaProfile();
    profile.preferences().set("Geolocation",
      Enable geolocation", false);
    driver = new OperaDriver(profile);
    driver.get("http://book.theautomatedtester.co.uk/");

  }

  @After
  public void tearDown(){
    driver.quit();
  }

  @Test
  public void testExamples(){
    WebElement element = driver.findElement(
      By.linkText("Chapter 4"));
    element.click();
```

```
      Assert.assertEquals(1, driver.findElements(
        By.linkText("index")).size());
    }
  }
```

What just happened?

We have just seen how we can set a preference with Opera and then inject that into the browser so that when the browser starts, it is there for us to use. As mentioned earlier, there are a lot of different preferences that can be set. To see a list of these, open Opera and use the URL `opera:config` or visit `http://www.opera.com/support/usingopera/operaini/`.

Pop quiz – working with OperaDriver

1. What version is recommended for use with OperaDriver?

2. How do we update the browser preference with OperaDriver?

Working with InternetExplorerDriver

Internet Explorer is the most used browser in the world followed by Firefox and Google Chrome so getting IEDriver working is going to be a high priority. The current version IEDriver supports IE6 through to IE9 so you will be able to test your websites work on old browsers right up to the latest modern version of the browser.

If you haven't downloaded the IEDriverServer you will need to do it now for the following section. You will also need to set an environment path of where it is so InternetExplorerDriver in Java will know where to get it. This is similar to what we did for the ChromeDriver earlier.

On Windows do: `set PATH=$PATH;\path\to\chromedriver`.

Time for action – working with Internet Explorer

In this section we are going to get the text of the element on the page. This is something that most people have to do to check that the right things are happening on the page.

We will need to instantiate InternetExplorerDriver and the call getText() on the element. Let's get to it.

1. Update the setUp() method to load InternetExplorerDriver():

```
driver = new InternetExplorerDriver();
```

2. Now we need to find an element. In this section we will find the link Chapter 4:

```
WebElement element = driver.findElement(By.id("bid"));
```

3. Now we need to get the text of the element:

```
element.getText();
```

4. Run your test and it should look like the following:

```
public class TestChapter6 {

   WebDriver driver;

   @Before
   public void setUp(){
      driver = new InternetExplorerDriver();
      driver.get("http://book.theautomatedtester.co.uk/chapter4");

   }

   @After
   public void tearDown(){
    driver.quit();
   }

   @Test
   public void testExamples(){
      WebElement element = driver.findElement(By.id("bid"));
      Assert.assertEquals("50", element.getText());
   }
}
```

What just happened?

We have just seen how we can use WebDriver to drive Internet Explorer. Since this is the most used browser in the world, we always make sure that our applications work with it. As with all of the different browsers, using Internet Explorer with WebDriver is really simple.

Pop quiz – working with InternetExplorerDriver

1.   What versions of Internet Explorer does WebDriver support?

Other important points

You will notice that in the `tearDown()` we call `quit()`. We call `quit()` because this call cleans up all of the resources that WebDriver starts up and uses. If you were to call `close()` it will only close the window that Selenium WebDriver is currently on. On some implementations of the server-side, or browser code, when we `close()` and it is the last window open then the server-side code will act as though `quit()` was called.

Summary

We learnt a lot in this chapter about Selenium WebDriver and all of the different browsers that it supports and how we can use them.

Specifically, we covered:

♦   **FirefoxDriver**: We saw how easy it is to get started with WebDriver and Firefox and how we can go about setting preferences and installing add-ons. We also saw how we can tell FirefoxDriver where to launch Firefox from.

♦   **ChromeDriver**: We saw how easy it was to use ChromeDriver. Once we added the ChromeDriver executable that we downloaded to our PATH environment variable we were able to use the driver. We also saw how we can tweak settings before the browser loads if we wanted to install extensions or if we wanted to set the location of the Chromium Binary.

♦   **OperaDriver**: In this section we learnt how to use OperaDriver to work against our web application. We were also able to change preferences of the browser before it loaded so that we can try and test it as users would use it.

♦   **InternetExplorerDriver**: In this section we saw how we can use InternetExplorerDriver to drive Internet Explorer. We need to make sure that our applications work in Internet Explorer since it has the largest market share so getting this right is useful.

We also discussed calling `quit()` when we are finished with WebDriver so that it can clean up resources.

Now that we've learnt about desktop browsers, we're ready to learn about mobile browsers—which is the topic of the next chapter.

7
Mobile Devices

We are currently seeing an explosion of mobile devices to the market. A lot of them are more powerful than your average computer was just over a decade ago. This means that in addition to having nice clean, responsive, and functional desktop applications, we are starting to have to make sure the same basic functionality is available to mobile devices. In this chapter, we are going to be looking at how we can set up mobile devices to be used with Selenium WebDriver.

In this chapter, we shall learn:

- How to use the stock browser on Android
- How to test with Opera Mobile
- How to test on iOS

So let's get on with it...

Important preliminary points

While you can use the Android emulator for the Android parts of the chapter, it is highly recommended that you have a real device that you can use. The reason is that the emulator tries to emulate the hardware that phones run on. This means that it needs to translate it to a low-level command that ARM-based devices would understand. A real iOS device is not needed as that simulates a device and therefore is significantly faster. The device will also need to have Android 4.0+ or better known as Ice Cream Sandwich. You will need to download the Android App from `http://code.google.com/p/selenium/downloads/list`. It will be named `android-server-<version>.apk` where `<version>` is the latest version.

You will however need to have a machine with OS X on to start the simulator since it is part of XCode. If you do not have XCode installed you can download it via the AppStore. You will also need to install all of the command-line tools that come with XCode. You will also need to check out the Selenium code from its source repository. You need to build the WebDriver code for iOS since it can't be added to the Apple App Store to be downloaded on to devices.

Working with Android

Android devices are becoming commonplace with owners of smartphones and tablets. This is because there are a number of handset providers in the market. This has meant that in some parts of the world, it is the only way that some people can access the Internet. With this in mind, we need to make sure that we can test the functionality.

Emulator

While it is not recommended to use the emulator due to the speed of it, it can be really useful. Since it will act like a real device in that it will run all the bits of code that we want on the virtual device, we can see how a web application will react.

Time for action – creating an emulator

If you do not have an Android device that you can use for testing, then you can set up an Android emulator. The emulator will then get the Selenium WebDriver APK installed and then that will control the browser on the device. Before we start, you will need to download the Android SDK from `http://developer.android.com/sdk/index.html`.

1. Open up a command prompt or a terminal.
2. Enter `cd <path>/android-sdk/tools` where `<path>` is the path to the `android-sdk` directory.
3. Now enter `./android create avd -n my_android -t 14` where:
    - `-n my_android` gives the emulator the name `my_android`.
    - `-t 14` tells it which version of android to use. `14` and higher is Android 4 and higher support.
4. When prompted **Do you wish to create a custom hardware profile [no]**, enter **no**.
5. Run the emulator with:
    ```
    ./emulator -avd my_android &
    ```

It will take some time to come up but once it has been started, you will not have to restart unless it crashes or you purposefully close it. Once loaded you should see something like the following:

What just happened?

We have just seen what is involved in setting up the Android emulator that we can use for testing of mobile versions of our applications. As was mentioned, we need to make sure that we set up the emulator to work with Android 4.0 or later. For the emulator we need to have a target platform of 14 or later. Now that we have this done, we can have a look at installing the WebDriver Server on the device.

Installing the Selenium WebDriver Android Server

We have seen that we can access different machines and control the browsers on those machines with Selenium WebDriver RemoteDriver. We need to do the same with Android. The APK file that you downloaded earlier is the Selenium Server that is specifically designed for Android devices. It has a smaller memory footprint since mobile devices do not have the same amount of memory as your desktop machine.

We need to install this on the emulator or the physical device that you have.

Time for action – installing the Android Server

In this section, we will learn the steps required to install the Android server on the device or emulator that you are going to be using. To do this, you will need to have downloaded the APK file from `http://code.google.com/p/selenium/downloads/list`. If you are installing this onto a real device make sure that you allow installs from **Unknown Sources**.

1. Open a command prompt or a terminal.

2. Start the emulator or device if you haven't already.

3. We need to run the available devices:

   ```
   <path to>/android_sdk/platform-tools/adb devices
   ```

4. It will look like this:

   ```
   * daemon not running. starting it now on port 5037 *
   * daemon started successfully *
   List of devices attached
   3930A259826000EC          device
   ```

5. Take the serial number of the device.

6. Now we need to install. We do that with the following command:

   ```
   adb -s <serialId> -e install -r  android-server.apk
   ```

7. Once that is done you will see this in the command prompt or terminal:

   ```
   3594 KB/s (1881490 bytes in 0.511s)
           pkg: /data/local/tmp/android-server-2.21.0.apk
   Success
   ```

8. And on the device you will see:

What just happened?

We have just seen how we can install the Android Server on the server. This process is useful for installing any Android app from the command line. Now that this is done we are ready to start looking at running some Selenium WebDriver code against the device.

Creating a test for Android

Now that we have looked at getting the device or emulator ready, we are ready to start creating a test that will work against a site. The good thing about the Selenium WebDriver, like Selenium RC, is that we can easily move from browser to browser with only a small change. In this section, we are going to be introduced to the AndroidDriver.

Time for action – using the Android driver

In this section we are going to be looking at running some tests against an Android device or emulator. This should be a fairly simple change to our test, but there are a couple of things that we need to do right before the test runs.

1. Open a command prompt or terminal.

2. We need to start the server. We can do this by touching the app or we can do this from the command line with the following command:

   ```
   adb -s <serialId> shell am start -a android.intent.action.MAIN -n
   org.openqa.selenium.android.app/.MainActivity
   ```

3. We now need to forward all the HTTP traffic to the device or emulator. This means that all the JSON Wire Protocol calls, that we learnt earlier, go to the device. We do it with:

```
adb -s <serialId> forward tcp:8080 tcp:8080
```

4. Now we are ready to update our test. I will show an example from the previous test:

```
import junit.framework.TestCase;

import org.openqa.selenium.By;
import org.openqa.selenium.WebElement;
import org.openqa.selenium.android.AndroidDriver;


public class TestChapter7 {

  WebDriver driver;

  @Before
  public void setUp(){
    driver = new AndroidDriver();
    driver.get("http://book.theautomatedtester.co.uk/chapter4");
  }

  @After
  public void tearDown(){
    driver.quit();
  }

  @Test
  public void testExamples(){
    WebElement element = driver.findElement(By.id("nextBid"));
    element.sendKeys("100");
  }
}
```

5. Run the test. You will see that it runs the same test against the Android device. In the previous chapter we had this work against desktop browsers.

What just happened?

We have just run our first test against an Android device. We saw that we had to forward the HTTP traffic to port 8080 to the device. This means that the normal calls, which use the JSON Wire Protocol, will then be run on the device.

Currently Opera Software is working on getting OperaDriver to work on Mobile devices. There are a few technical details that are being worked on and hopefully in the future we will be able to use it.

Mozilla is also working on their solution for Mobile with Selenium. Currently a project called Marionette is being worked on that allows Selenium to work on Firefox OS, Firefox Mobile for Android as well as Firefox for Desktop. You can read up on it at `https://wiki.mozilla.org/Auto-tools/Projects/Marionette`.

Pop quiz – working with Android

1. How do we set up an Android emulated device for our tests?
2. How do you see which devices are connected to the host?
    a. adb devices
    b. Adb phones
    c. Adb handsets
3. How do you install the APK on the device or emulator?
    a. `adb -s <serialId> -e install -r android-server.apk`
    b. Install it from `http://code.google.com/p/selenium/downloads/list`
    c. both
4. How do you start the App on the emulator or device without touching it?
5. How do I forward the HTTP traffic to the device?

    a. `Abd -s <serialId> redirect tcp:8080 tcp:8080`
    b. `Abd -s <serialId> redirect tcp:8080 tcp:8080`
    c. `adb -s <serialId> forward tcp:8080 tcp:8080`

Have a go hero – updating tests for Android

Have a look at updating all of the tests that you would have written so far in the book to run on Android. It should not take you long to update them.

Running with OperaDriver on a mobile device

In this section we are going to have a look at using the OperaDriver, the Selenium WebDriver object to control Opera, in order to drive Opera Mobile. Opera has a large market share on mobile devices especially on lower end Android devices.

Before we start we are going to need to download a special emulator for Opera Mobile.

 As of writing this, it has just come out of Opera's Labs so the download links may have been updated.

Windows: http://www.opera.com/download/get.pl?id=34969&sub=true&nothan ks=yes&location=360.

Mac: http://www.opera.com/download/get.pl?id=34970&sub=true&nothanks=y es&location=360.

Linux 64 Bit: Deb: http://www.opera.com/download/get.pl?id=34967&sub=true& nothanks=yes&location=360.

Tarball: http://www.opera.com/download/get.pl?id=34968&sub=true&nothanks =yes&location=360.

Linux 32 Bit: Deb: http://www.opera.com/download/get.pl?id=34965&sub=true& nothanks=yes&location=360.

TarBall: http://www.opera.com/download/get.pl?id=34966&sub=true&nothanks =yes&location=360.

Let's now see this in action.

Time for action – using OperaDriver on Opera Mobile

To make sure that we have the right amount of coverage over the browsers that users may be using, there is a good chance that you will need to add Opera Mobile. Before starting, make sure that you have downloaded the version of the emulator for your Operating System with one of the links mentioned previously.

1. Create a new test file. Add the following code to it:

```
import junit.framework.TestCase;

import org.openqa.selenium.By;
import org.openqa.selenium.WebElement;

public class TestChapter7OperaMobile{
  WebDriver driver;
}
```

2. What we now need to do is add a setup method. We will have to add a couple of items to our DesiredCapabilities object. This will tell OperaDriver that we want to work against a mobile version.

```
@Before
public void setUp(){
   DesiredCapabilities c = DesiredCapabilities.opera();
   c.setCapability("opera.product", OperaProduct.MOBILE);
   c.setCapability("opera.binary",
     "/path/to/my/custom/opera-mobile-build");

   driver = new OperaDriver(c);
     }
```

3. Now we can add a test to make sure that we have a working test again:

```
@Test
public void testShouldLoadGoogle() {
   driver.get("http://www.google.com");
   //Let's find an element to see if it works
   driver.findElement(By.name("q"));
}
```

4. Let's now add a teardown:

```
@After
public void teardown(){
   driver.quit();
}
```

5. Your class altogether should look like the following:

```
import junit.framework.TestCase;

import org.openqa.selenium.By;
import org.openqa.selenium.WebElement;

public class TestChapter7OperaMobile{
   WebDriver driver;

   @Before
   public void setUp(){
     DesiredCapabilities c = DesiredCapabilities.opera();
     c.setCapability("opera.product", OperaProduct.MOBILE);
     c.setCapability("opera.binary",
       "/path/to/my/custom/opera-mobile-build");

     driver = new OperaDriver(c);
```

```
      }

      @After
      public void teardown(){
        driver.quit();
      }
      @Test
      public void testShouldLoadGoogle() {
        driver.get("http://book.theautomatedtester.co.uk");


      }
    }
```

6. And the following should appear in your emulator:

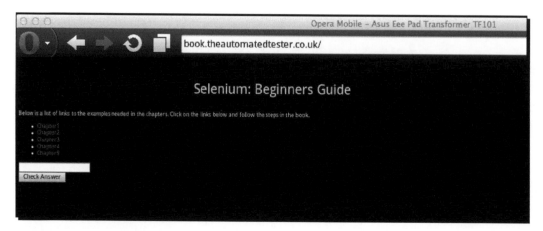

What just happened?

We have just seen what is required to run a test against Opera Mobile using OperaDriver. This uses the same communication layer that is used in communicating with the Opera desktop browser called Scope.

We will see the mobile versions of web applications, if they are available, and be able to interact with them.

If you would like the OperaDriver to load up tablet size UI, then you can add the following to use the tablet UI with a display of 1280x800 pixels. This is a common size for tablets that are currently on the market.

```
    c.setCapability("opera.arguments",
      "-tabletui -displaysize 1280x800");
```

If you want to see the current orientation of the device and to access the touch screen elements, you can swap OperaDriver object for OperaDriverMobile. For the most part, you should be able to do nearly all of your work against the normal driver.

Working with iOS

iPhones and iPod Touches are such commonplace these days. A lot of companies are working hard to offer a really good experience for these users. This means that users are starting to become accustomed to using web applications with their phones.

We can run our tests against the simulator or against the real device. Compared to Android, the simulator is really quick. This is because it is not trying to emulate the hardware of actual Apple devices.

Time for action – setting up the simulator

In this section, we are going to be making sure that we have the simulator or device ready. To do this we will need to do the following:

1. If you haven't checked the Selenium Code out, follow the steps at `http://code.google.com/p/selenium/source/checkout`.

2. Open `selenium/iphone/iWebDriver.xcodeproj` in XCode.

3. If you want to build it for the simulator, set your build configuration to **Simulator / iPad OS 5.0 / iWebDriver**. This is done in a drop-down box in the top-left of the project window.

4. Click **Build & Go**! iWebDriver will be built and the simulator will start. You can see what it will look like in the following screenshot:

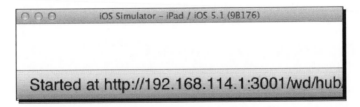

What just happened?

We have just got all the requirements ready to start writing our first test. After making sure that we have XCode, which has the iOS SDK, we were able to start the simulator and have iWebDriver installed.

We will now have a look at how to set up running your tests against a real device. Before we do that, we are going to have to make sure that we have set up a provisioning profile.

To do this we need to do the following. One thing to note is that you will have to pay US$99 to join the iOS program. To do this:

1. Get a developer account from Apple. This is done at `https://developer.apple.com`.

2. Create a certificate signing request.

3. Open **Keychain Access**:

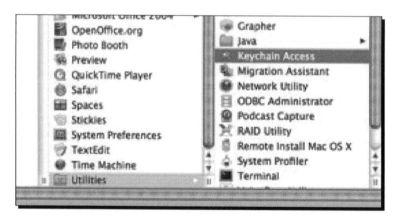

4. Request a Certificate from a certificate authority by doing **Keychain Access | Certificate Assistant | Request a Certificate From a Certificate Authority**:

5. Complete the form as show in the following screenshot:

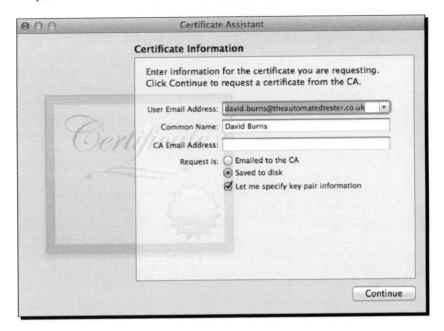

6. Click **Continue** and then save the file to somewhere that you will be able to access it:

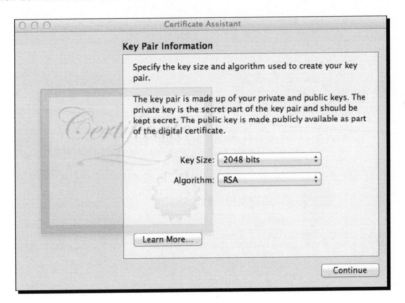

7. Click **Continue** and then it should say that it was successful as shown in the following screenshot:

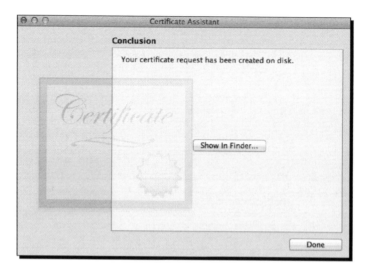

8. Go to the iPhone Developer Program Portal on `https://developer.apple.com`.

9. Launch the **Assistant** as in the following screenshot:

10. Go through the **Provisioning Assistant** and complete all the steps that you are asked to do:

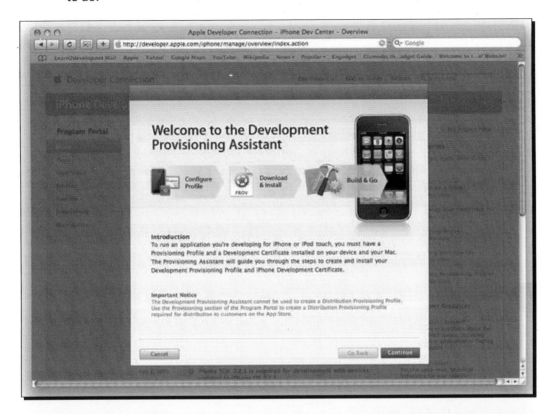

Time for action – setting up on a real device

Setting up tests to run on a simulator is quite useful but having the tests running on a mobile device can be really useful. Let us have a look at setting this up on a real mobile device:

1. You will also need a provisioning profile from Apple to be installed and configured for your device.

2. Open `Info.plist` and edit the `Bundle Identifier` to `com.NAME.$ {PRODUCT_NAME:identifier}` where `NAME` is the name you registered your provisioning profile to be an authority on.

3. Make sure your device is connected to your computer. Your device must also be routable from your computer. The easiest way to do this is to configure a wifi network and connect your device to it.

4. Click **Build & Go**. iWebDriver will be installed on the device.

What just happened?

We have just installed iWebDriver on a real device. We can now run our tests against iPhones or iPads. The hard part in running tests against these devices is now done. Let's have a look at updating our tests.

Creating a test for iOS devices

Now that we have looked at getting the device or simulator ready, we are ready to start creating a test that will work against a site. The good thing about the Selenium WebDriver, like Selenium RC, is that we can easily move from browser to browser with only a small change. In this section, we are going to be introduced to the iPhoneDriver.

Time for action – using the iPhone driver

In this section, we are going to be looking at running some tests against an iOS device or simulator. This should be a fairly simple change to our test but there are a couple of things that we need to do right before the test runs.

1. Now we are ready to update our test. I will show an example from the previous test:

```
import junit.framework.TestCase;

import org.openqa.selenium.By;
import org.openqa.selenium.WebElement;
import org.openqa.selenium.iphone.IphoneDriver;


public class TestChapter7 {

  WebDriver driver;

  @Before
  public void setUp(){
    driver = new IPhoneDriver();
    driver.get("http://book.theautomatedtester.co.uk/chapter4");
  }

  @After
  public void tearDown(){
    driver.quit();
  }

  @Test
  public void testExamples(){
```

```
        WebElement element = driver.findElement(By.id("nextBid"));
        element.sendKeys("100");
    }
}
```

2. Run the test. You will see that it runs the same test against an iOS device. In the previous chapter we had this work against desktop browsers.

What just happened?

We have just seen how we can run our tests against iOS devices. Depending on which simulator we start XCode from, we can either have it run against iPhone or iPad.

Have a go hero – updating tests for iOS Devices

Have a look at updating all of the tests that you would have written so far in the book to run on iOS. It should not take you long to update them.

Summary

We learnt a lot in this chapter about using Selenium WebDriver with mobile devices. We saw that after a little setup of the device and the machine running the test, it was fairly easy to get up and running.

Specifically, we covered:

◆   **Working with Android**: In this section we had a look at what is needed to set up Android for testing with Selenium WebDriver. We set up an emulator in case we didn't have a real device. We also saw how we can install the Android Server on the device or emulator.

   We then moved on to creating our test that ran against the emulator or the device.

◆   **Working with iOS**: In this section we looked at setting up the simulator or getting iWebDriver installed on a real device.

Now that we've learnt about mobile web testing, let's have a look at really setting up Selenium grid—which is the topic of the next chapter.

8

Getting Started with Selenium Grid

In this chapter we are going to have a look at what is Selenium Grid and how we can set it up on different environments. This will abstract the topography of where the tests are located so that your tests only have to worry about one address.

In this chapter, we shall learn:

- ◆ Setting up the Selenium Grid Hub
- ◆ Setting up the Selenium Grid Remote Controls
- ◆ Creating tests for the grid
- ◆ Running tests in parallel

So let's get on with it...

 Please make sure that you download the latest Selenium Server from `http://seleniumhq.org/download`.

Understanding Selenium Grid

Selenium Grid is a version of Selenium that allows teams to set up a number of Selenium instances and then have one central point to send your Selenium commands to. This differs from what we saw in Selenium RemoteWebDriver where we always had to explicitly say where the Selenium Server is as well as know what browsers that server can handle.

With Selenium Grid we just ask for a specific browser, and then the hub that is part of Selenium Grid will route all the Selenium commands through to the Remote Control you want.

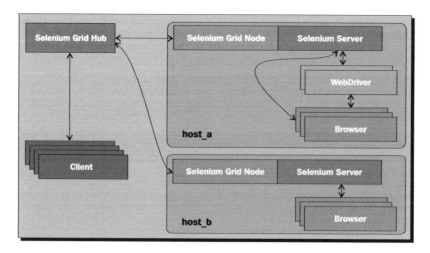

Selenium Grid also allows us to call a specific browser on a specific platform with just a simple update to the desired capabilities object that we learnt about in previous chapters. This allows us to route our tests accordingly so that we know that we are testing on the right browser on the right platform. We can see an example of this in the following screenshot:

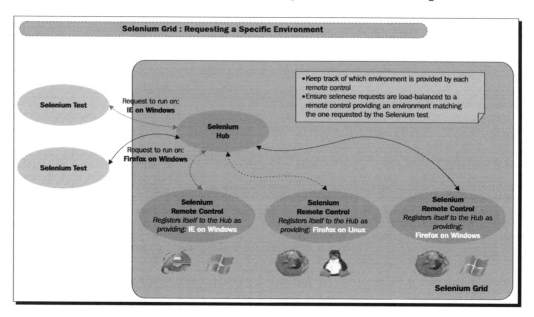

We will see how to create tests for this later in the chapter but for now let's have a look at making sure we have all the necessary items ready for the grid.

We are now ready to start setting up the grid.

Selenium Grid Hub

Selenium Grid works by having a central point that tests can connect to, and then commands are pushed to Selenium Server nodes that are connected to the hub. The hub has a web interface that tells you about the Selenium Server and the browser instances connected to the hub and if they are currently in use.

Time for action – launching the hub

Now that we are ready to start working with Selenium Grid, we need to set up the grid. This is a simple command that we run in the console or command prompt.

1. Open a command prompt or console.

2. Run the command:

   ```
   java -jar selenium-server-standalone-x.xx.xx.jar -role hub
   ```

3. When that command executes, you should see something like the following screenshot:

4. We can see that this is running in the command prompt or console. We can also see the hub running from within a browser.

5. We can enter `http://nameofmachine:4444/grid/console` where `nameofmachine` is the name of the machine with the hub. If it is on your machine, then you can enter `http://localhost:4444/grid/console`. We can see a screenshot of that:

What just happened?

We have successfully started Selenium Grid Hub. This is the central point of our tests and Selenium Grid instances. We saw that when we start Selenium Grid it showed us what items were available according to the configuration file that is with the normal install. One thing to note is that if you need to change the port, you can pass in `-port ####`. Just replace the `####` with the port number that you wish to use.

We then had a look at how we can see what the grid is doing by having a look at the hub in a browser. We did this by putting the URL `http://nameofmachine:4444/grid/console` where `nameofmachine` is the name of the machine that we would like to access with the hub. It shows what configured environments the hub can handle, what grid instances are available, and which instances are currently active.

Now that we have the hub ready we can have a look at starting up instances.

Adding instances to the hub

Now that we have successfully started the Selenium Grid hub, we will need to have a look at how we can start adding Selenium servers to the hub so it starts forming the grid of computers that we are expecting. You will notice that compared to Selenium Grid for Selenium 1, we won't have to be adding a new server for each browser that we want to use. The server has always been able to handle more than one browser and because of architectural changes, we can now start one server and have it control all the browsers installed on that machine.

Time for action – adding a server with the defaults

In this section we are going to launch Selenium server and get it to register with the hub. We are going to assume that the browser on which you would like to register all known browsers and the hub are on the same machine as the grid node. We will pass in two required arguments which are: the server we are starting is a node and where the hub is. The selenium server will try and use port 5555. If that is not available you will get an error saying that the port is already in use. We can, and will in a future section, see how you can set the port manually.

1. Open command prompt or console.

2. Enter the command `java -jar selenium-server-standalone..jar -role node -hub http://localhost:4444/grid/register` and press return. You should see the following in your command prompt or console:

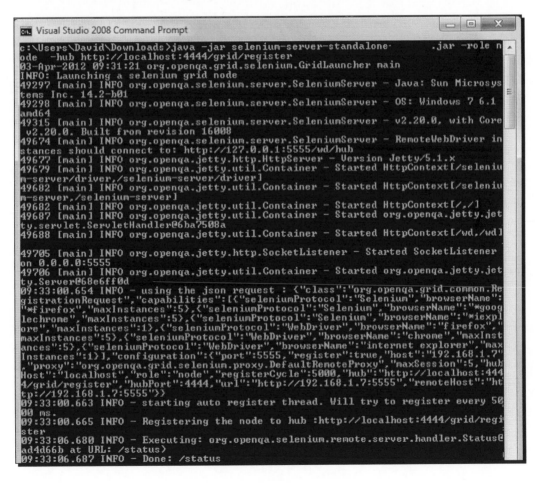

3. And this in the Selenium Grid Hub site:

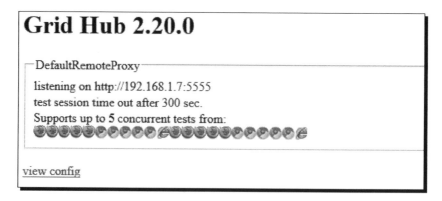

What just happened?

We have added our first machine to our own Selenium Grid. It has used all the defaults that are available. It has created a Selenium Server that will take any Firefox, Google Chrome, and in this case Internet Explorer requests and is on the same machine as the host of Selenium server grid. This is a useful way to set up the grid really quickly with all the default browsers.

Adding Selenium Remote Controls for different machines

Selenium Grid is most powerful when you can add it to multiple operating systems. This allows us to check that, for instance, whether Firefox on Windows and Firefox on Linux is doing the same thing during a test. To register new remote controls to the grid from a machine other than the one hosting the hub, we need to tell it where the hub is.

Let's see this in action.

Time for action – adding Selenium server for different machines

For this section, you will need to have another machine available for you to use. This could be the Ubuntu machine that you needed for the previous chapter. If you have a small grid, then you can name them according to the operating system that it is run on.

1. Open a command prompt or console.

2. Run the command `java -jar selenium-server-standalone.jar -role node -hub http://<name of server>:4444/grid/register`.

3. When you have run this your grid site should look like the following:

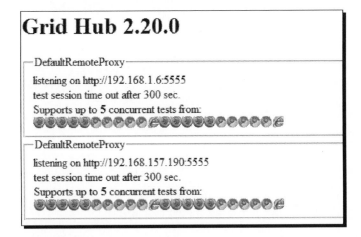

What just happened?

We have added a new remote control to the grid from a machine other than where the Selenium Grid Hub is running. This is the first time that we have been able to set up our remote control instances in a grid. We learnt about the −hub argument that is needed when launching the selenium server. We then saw that it has updated the grid site that is running on the hub.

Now that we have this working as we expected, let us have a look at setting up the server to do specific tasks.

Adding Selenium server to do specific browser tasks on specific operating systems

Selenium Grid is extremely powerful when we start using different browsers on the grid, since we can't run all the different browsers on a single machine due to operating systems and browser combinations. There is currently up to nine different combinations that are used by most people, so getting Selenium Grid to help with this can give you the test coverage that you need.

To do this we pass in the −browser argument in a command line call. Let us see how we can set the items.

Time for action – setting the environment when starting Selenium Remote Control

Now that we need to get Internet Explorer Selenium Remote Controls added to our grid, we have to add the `-browser` argument to our call with the target on the configured environments. Since we want to use Internet Explorer, we can use the IE on Windows target.

1. Open a console or command prompt.

2. Run the command:

```
java -jar selenium-server-standalone.jar -role node  -hub http://
localhost:4444/grid/register -browser browserName="internet explor
er",maxInstances=1,platform=WINDOWS
```

3. When it is running your hub page should look like this:

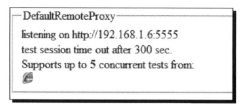

What just happened?

We have just seen how we can create grid nodes to only have the browsers that we want. We chose Internet Explorer but we could also choose Firefox, Google Chrome, or Opera. This is quite useful when we need to test a large amount of browser and operating system combinations. If you enter `-browser` on the command line, it will add those browsers too.

Using Selenium Grid 2 with your YAML file

If you have been using Selenium Grid from Selenium 1, you will have set up your YAML file. This can now be used with Selenium by passing in a file like the following one. To do this we just need to pass in a new argument called `-grid1Yml`:

```
hub:
  port: 4444
  remoteControlPollingIntervalInSeconds: 180
  sessionMaxIdleTimeInSeconds: 300
  environments:
    - name:     "Firefox on Windows"
      browser: "*firefox"
```

Let's see this in action.

Time for action – using Selenium Grid 1 configuration

A number of us have set up a Selenium Grid using the Selenium 1 Grid and have been using it for a long time. Since we have this why not upgrade the nodes to the Selenium Server that supports both Remote Control and WebDriver and use our original configuration? One thing to note is that we will only be able to run Selenium Remote Control tests this way.

Let's have a try at starting this all up.

1. Open a console or command prompt.

2. Run the command:

   ```
   java -jar selenium-server-standalone.jar -role hub -grid1Yml
   selenium-grid-1.0.8/grid_configuration.yml
   ```

3. If we have a look at the grid config page by clicking the view config link, then we will see it in there:

```
port : 4444
prioritizer : null
servlets : []
throwOnCapabilityNotPresent : true
timeout : 300000

updated with grid1 config :selenium-grid-1.0.8/grid_configuration.yml
host : null
port : 4444
cleanUpCycle : 180000
timeout : 300000
newSessionWaitTimeout : -1
grid1Mapping : {*firefox3=*firefox3, Safari on OS X=*safari, *chrome=*chrome,
*firefox2=*firefox2, Google Chrome on Windows=*googlechrome,
*firefoxproxy=*firefoxproxy, *pifirefox=*pifirefox, Firefox on Windows=*firefox,
*iehta=*iehta, *piiexplore=*piiexplore, *iexploreproxy=*iexploreproxy, *opera=*opera,
Google Chrome on Linux=*googlechrome, Firefox on OS X=*firefox,
```

What just happened?

We have just got the Selenium Grid to load our original Selenium Grid item by passing in the original YAML file. This then gets used by the hub once it has started up!

Pop quiz – using Selenium Grid 2

1. What is the command required to start the Hub?

2. What is the URL where one can see what is happening on the grid?

3. How do you specify the port the remote control is running on?

4. How do you specify which browser you would like the remote control to be registered with?

Running tests against the grid

Now that we have set up the grid with different instances, we should have a look at how we can write tests against these remote controls on the grid. We can pass in the value of the target that we can see in the grid and then run the tests. So instead of passing in the standard desired capabilities, you can be more specific and the grid hub will route data so you can then run the tests as normal. Let's see this in action.

Time for action – writing tests against the grid

Now that we have a Selenium Grid set up we need to write a test that works against the grid. Working against Selenium grid is exactly the same as working with Selenium WebDrive's RemoteWebDriver. The Selenium Grid will find the relevant node and route all the commands to be executed there.

1. Create a new test file.

2. Populate it with a test script that accesses an item on the grid and then works against http://book.theautomatedtester.co.uk/. Your script should look something like the following:

```
import org.junit.*;
import org.openqa.selenium.*;
import org.openqa.selenium.firefox.*;

import java.io.File;
import java.util.Dictionary;

public class TestExample1 {

  WebDriver driver;

  @Before
  public void setUp(){
    DesiredCapabilities capability =
      DesiredCapabilities.firefox();
```

```
        capability.setBrowserName("firefox" );
        // Set the platform we want our tests to run on
        capability.setPlatform("LINUX");
        driver = new RemoteWebDriver(new URL(
           "http://<grid hub>:4444/wd/hub"), capability);

        driver.get("http://book.theautomatedtester.co.uk/chapter1");
    }

    @After
    public void tearDown(){
       driver.quit();
    }

    @Test
    public void testExamples(){
       // We will put examples in here
    }
```

What just happened?

We have just seen how we can write tests that can run against the grid and then run them. When the tests are running, the grid will show which browsers are currently in use and which grid items are currently free.

Running tests in parallel

So far we have managed to get our tests cycling through different machines. We have also got it working against the Selenium Grid hub so we can see all of our tests being split out to the machines that we make sure that we test against browser and operating system combinations.

In this section, we will look at how we can add a thread-count attribute to the `<suite>` node in our test configuration file. We also will need to add the parallel attribute to the test suite. The value that it takes will either be methods or classes. This will mean that either the methods, the test cases, are run in parallel or the classes that contain the test cases are running in parallel.

Time for action – getting our tests running in parallel

Now we are ready to start having our tests running in parallel.

1. Open your `TestNG` XML configuration file.

2. Add `parallel=methods` to the suite node.

3. Add `thread-count=3` to the suite node. This will run your tests with three threads. This number can be any value that you want. It is best practice to only let this number go to the number of cores that the machine running the tests has minus the number of Selenium Remote Controls running.

4. Right-click on the configuration file in IDEA and run the tests.

What just happened?

We have just managed to get our tests running in parallel. As you can see this has been fairly easy. We saw that adding the parallel and the thread-count attributes allows us to run these tests in parallel and when coupled with Selenium Grid we can start to get our tests running near 1/n which is where we want our tests to be.

Summary

We learnt a lot in this chapter about how we can set up Selenium Grid and all the different arguments needed as well as running our tests against the grid.

Specifically, we covered:

- **Starting the Selenium Grid Hub**: In this section of the book we had a look at how we can start up the Selenium Grid Hub that is the central point for Selenium Grid.

- **Setting up Selenium Grid Nodes**: We had a look at all the arguments that are needed to add a Selenium server to the grid so that we can use it. This gives us a more manageable view of our grid so that we can work with it.

- **Running tests in parallel**: In this section we learnt how we can run our tests in parallel. We also had a look at how we can cycle through different browsers using the `@Parameter` annotation.

We also discussed how we can create tests that use the grid.

Now that we've learnt about setting up Selenium Grid and have looked into getting our test time down by running things in parallel using Selenium Grid, let's have a look at using Selenium to do more advanced user interactions—which is the topic of the next chapter.

9

Advanced User Interactions

As we have seen, clicking and typing is quite straightforward with Selenium WebDriver. Find the element and then interact with it. Unfortunately a lot of the modern web applications that are being created are a lot more than just typing and clicking. In this chapter, we will have a look at how we can drag and drop and move the mouse to specific places on the page.

In this chapter, we shall learn:

◆ What is the Advanced User Interactions API

◆ Building up a sequence of actions and performing them

So let's get on with it...

Important preliminary points

You will need to have the currently released version of Firefox or the version before that for this section of the book. You will also need to do this chapter on Microsoft Windows or a Linux distribution. This is required so that we can do native interactions. Native interactions inject events into the browser just like if you were typing on a keyboard. You will be able to do this chapter on a Mac OS X. Selenium WebDriver will use synthetic events by injecting events onto the page via JavaScript.

What is the Advanced User Interactions

The Advanced User Interactions API is a new, more comprehensive API for describing actions a user can perform on a web page. Normally we need to find elements and then send actions through them. If we need to perform complex tasks like hold down *Control* and click, then this may not work.

The Advanced User Interactions allows us to build these complex interactions with elements in a really nice API. The API relies on two key interfaces for this to work.

Keyboard

The keyboard interface allows keys to be pressed, held down, and released. It also allows for normal typing.

Methods available are:

- `void sendKeys(CharSequence... keysToSend)`: Similar to the existing `sendKeys(...)` method.

- `void pressKey(Keys keyToPress)`: Sends a key press only, without releasing it. Should only be implemented for modifier keys (*Control*, *Alt*, and *Shift*).

- `void releaseKey(Keys keyToRelease)`: Releases a modifier key.

Mouse

The mouse interface allows for mouse clicks, double clicks, context clicks, as well as moving the mouse to a specific point or to a specific element on the page.

Methods available are:

- `void click(WebElement onElement)`: Similar to the existing `click()` method

- `void doubleClick(WebElement onElement)`: Double-clicks an element

- `void mouseDown(WebElement onElement)`: Holds down the left mouse button on an element

- `void mouseUp(WebElement onElement)`: Releases the mouse button on an element

- `void mouseMove(WebElement toElement)`: Move (from the current location) to another element

- ◆ void mouseMove(WebElement toElement, long xOffset, long yOffset): Move (from the current location) to new coordinates (X coordinates of toElement + xOffset, Y coordinates of toElement + yOffset)

- ◆ void contextClick(WebElement onElement): Performs a context-click (right-click) on an element

These methods are useful to know but when working and creating a sequence of it, it is better to use the Actions chain generator and then call perform on that class.

This is the next section of the chapter.

Actions

The Actions class allows us to build a chain of actions that we would like to perform. This means that we can build up a nice sequence, for example "Press *Shift* and type and then release", or if we wanted to work with a select that allows multiple selects, we could press *Shift* and then do the necessary clicks.

We do this by creating an Actions object. We then need to chain some calls together:

```
// Create Actions object passing in a WebDriver object
Actions builder = new Actions(driver);

// Chain some calls together and call build
Action dragAndDrop = builder.clickAndHold(someElement)
    .moveToElement(otherElement)
    .release(otherElement)
    .build();

// Perform the actions
dragAndDrop.perform();
```

Drag and drop

We have seen that drag and drop is one of the main things that people want to do with web applications. This allows them to build task boards that allow people to drag and drop between different states. You may have seen applications like this if you work in an Agile environment.

Let's try and create a basic drag and drop example using the little bit we already know of the Actions class.

Time for action – creating an Actions chain for dragging and dropping

A lot of web applications these days allow users to drag and drop what they want where they want on the page. This is really nice from a usability point of view, but from a testability point it is a nightmare!

We can get around this with actions API.

1. Open up inteliij and create a new Selenium WebDriver project.

2. Create a new class and a new test with the following code:

```
WebDriver driver = new FirefoxDriver();
driver.get("http://www.theautomatedtester.co.uk/demo2.html");
WebElement someElement =
    driver.findElement(By.className("draggable"));
WebElement otherElement =
    driver.findElement(By.className("droppable"));

Actions builder = new Actions(driver);
Action dragAndDrop = builder.clickAndHold(someElement)
    .moveToElement(otherElement)
    .release(otherElement)
    .build();

dragAndDrop.perform();
```

3. Run the test. You should see this first:

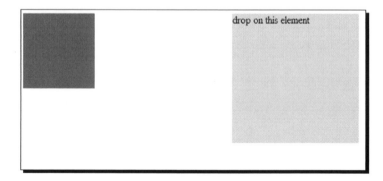

drop on this element

4. And when it is complete you will see the block go blue:

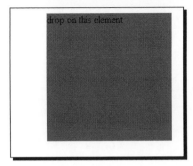

What just happened?

We have just seen how easy it is to do a drag and drop on the page. We just need to create an Actions object and then create a chain of events. When we have built up the chain we call `build()`. This puts everything in the right order and when we call `perform()`, the items are popped out of the queue and run in order.

Let us have a look at doing some slightly more complex chains with the Actions class.

Moving an element to an offset

We can get around this with the actions API.

Time for action – moving an element with a drag-and-drop by offset

There are times where we need to only move an image by a certain amount. A good example of this would be if you are working in a WYSIWYG editor and you wanted to just move an image to somewhere else but did not want to drop it on another element, you will be using `dragAndDropBy(WebElement, x, y);`.

Let us see this in action.

1. Open up inteliij and create a new Selenium WebDriver project.

2. Create a new class and a new test with the following code:

```
WebDriver driver = new FirefoxDriver();
driver.get("http://www.theautomatedtester.co.uk/demo2.html");
WebElement drag = driver.findElement(By.className("draggable"));

Actions builder = new Actions(driver);
```

```
Action dragAndDrop = builder.dragAndDropBy(drag, 10, 20)
    .build();

dragAndDrop.perform();
```

3. Run the test. You should see the following:

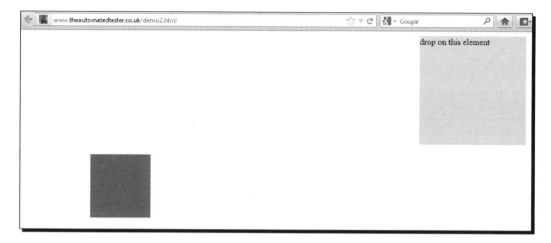

What just happened?

We have just seen how easy it is to do a drag-and-drop on the page by moving an item by an offset. You will have to pass in the element that you want to move and then the x and y offset that you want to move it by.

Doing a context click

If you are testing a highly rich application, like a WYSIWYG editor or an e-mail client, you will more than likely need to do a context click or right-click to get other menu items. This may seem like a simple task as a user but doing this within a browser and doing it programmatically has been a difficult task for some time. The interactions API allows us to do this and do it in a meaningful way.

We will now see it in action.

Time for action – doing a context click

If you are working in a document editor online or in an e-mail client and you are required to load a context menu, this will be useful. This can also be useful to load other bits of functionality or access specific pages.

To do this we will have to do the following:

1. Open up inteliij and create a new Selenium WebDriver project.

2. Create a new class and a new test with the following code:

```
WebDriver driver = new FirefoxDriver();
driver.get("http://www.theautomatedtester.co.uk/demo1.html");
Actions builder = new Actions(driver);
WebElement element = driver.findElement(By.tagName("body"));
Action contextClick = builder.contextClick(element)
    .build();

contextClick.perform();
```

3. Run the test. You should see the following:

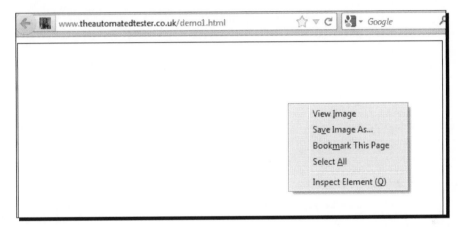

What just happened?

We have managed to get our code to cause a right-click to happen on the page. This means that we can now get to areas of our application that have overridden the default behavior. We see this happening in a lot of WYSIWYG editors and in really rich HTML web applications.

Clicking on multiple items in a select element

When filling in forms one of the nicest ways, and quickest way, to get information is to have a select that allows you to choose a number of items in the select. Unfortunately from a testing point of view this can be really hard to do since each click would just select a new item instead of keeping the last one.

Time for action – selecting multiple items on a select item

A number of forms nowadays ask users to select a number of items from a list.
For me a good example is the Advanced Search on Bugzilla. You can see an example at
`https://bugzilla.mozilla.org/query.cgi?format=advanced`. In Selenium
RC, selecting multiple items was impossible. Using the standard clicking and typing with
Selenium WebDriver we will not be able to do this either, however we can get around this
with the actions API.

1.   Open up inteliij and create a new Selenium WebDriver project.

2.   Create a new class and a new test with the following code:

```
WebDriver driver = new FirefoxDriver();
driver.get("http://book.theautomatedtester.co.uk/
multi-select.html");
Actions builder = new Actions(driver);
WebElement select = driver.findElement(
  By.tagName("select"));
List<WebElement> options = select.findElements(
  By.tagName("options"));
Action multipleSelect = builder.keyDown(Keys.SHIFT)
  .click(options.get(0))
  .click(options.get(2))
  .build();

multipleSelect.perform();
```

3.   Run the test. You should see the following:

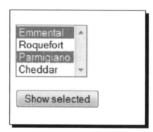

What just happened?

We have just successfully done a multi-select. This can be useful for testing forms that allow users to select multiple items. The same principle can be used if you needed to interact with anything that required both the keyboard and the mouse to be used at the same time.

Holding the mouse button down while moving the mouse

Canvas applications are becoming one of the most used HTML5 components to be added to applications. One of the nice things that we can do with it is draw pictures on the page just by clicking and holding down the mouse.

From the automation point of view, this would appear to be extremely difficult. We have commands like `click()` and we know that we can move an element by a specific offset but a `click()` doesn't do what we do.

Time for action – holding the mouse button down while moving the mouse

In this section we will have a look at how we can press down the left mouse button and then move it around the page. If you are working on a canvas that tracks the mouse movements, you would be able to draw a picture with the actions API. Let's see this in action:

1. Open up inteliij and create a new Selenium WebDriver project.

2. Create a new class and a new test with the following code:

```
WebDriver driver = new FirefoxDriver();
driver.get('http://www.theautomatedtester.co.uk/demo1.html')

Actions builder = new Actions(driver);
WebElement canvas = driver.findElement(By.id("tutorial"));
Action dragAndDrop = builder.clickAndHold(canvas)
   .moveByOffset(-40, -60)
   .moveByOffset(20, 20)
   .moveByOffset(100, 150)
   .release(canvas)
   .build();

dragAndDrop.perform();
```

3. Run the test. You should see the following:

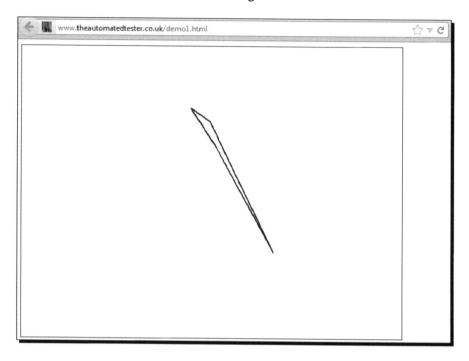

What just happened?

We have just seen how easy it is to hold the mouse button down and move it all over the page and then release the buttons. This type of action is one of the most complex types of work that we will have to do since it marries together a few.

Pop quiz – using Action Chains

1. What is the class that contains the action chain generator?

2. What is the method that builds up the chain?

3. What is the method that executes the chain in the order that it is created?

4. What is the best way to move the mouse by X coordinates to the side and Y coordinates up?

Summary

We have learnt a lot in this chapter about using the Advanced User Interactions API. We have seen how we can use it to work against web applications that have a large amount of key strokes or complex mouse movements.

Specifically, we covered:

- **What is the Advanced User API**: In this section we learnt what the API is and what makes it up. This is important since it sets us up for understanding the rest of the chapter.

- **Actions**: In this section we saw how we can start using the action chains to start building up complex chains of interactions with the page from typing to mouse movements. One thing to note is that the mouse won't appear to move but the right events will fire.

Now that we've learnt about Advanced User Interactions, we're finished learning all of the core aspects of Selenium. Now we can learn about good design patterns for writing tests—which is the topic of the next chapter.

10
Working with HTML5

HTML5 has become one of the latest buzzwords to hit web development in the last couple of years. With it has brought a number of useful items to web developers that make web applications act more like desktop applications. In this chapter, we will have a look at working with a number of the different technologies that cannot be accessed by normal clicking or typing.

In this chapter, we shall learn:

◆ Application cache

◆ Browser connections

◆ Web storage

So let's get on with it...

Important preliminary points

This only works with `AndroidDriver`, `IPhoneDriver`, and some of it works in Firefox. When working through the examples, we will need to make sure that we use those objects. We will be using the example class as follows:

```
import org.junit.*;
import org.openqa.selenium.*;

public class TestChapter10 {

    WebDriver driver;
```

```
@Before
public void setUp(){
   driver = new AndroidDriver();
   driver.get("http://book.theautomatedtester.co.uk/chapter4");
}

@After
public void tearDown(){
   driver.quit();
}

@Test
public void testExamples(){
   // We will put examples in here
}
}
```

Working with application cache

Application cache is one of the new technologies that is coming from the HTML 5 specification. It allows web applications to specify files that are downloaded when the browser accesses the page. The browser will look at the files in the application cache before opening any network connections to the server. This means if the computer or mobile device goes offline, then those files are still available and loaded straight away.

To know if your application has an application cache file, you will need to have a look at the source of the HTML document. It should have a manifest attribute in the html tag as follows:

```
<html manifest="example.appcache">
   ...
</html>
```

When items are downloaded, we can then make calls to the application cache object that is attached to the window object in the browser.

Selenium WebDriver has an AppCacheStatus enum that represents the current status of the application cache. The current statuses are:

- **0**: UNCACHED
- **1**: IDLE
- **2**: CHECKING
- **3**: DOWNLOADING

- ◆ **4**: UPDATEREADY
- ◆ **5**: OBSOLETE

Let's try using this.

Time for action – getting the current status of application cache

One of the things that you will want to constantly do during your testing is to make sure that the application cache is storing your files. We can see if they have been downloaded.

1. Create a new test class using the example code at the beginning of the chapter.

2. In this part we are just going to check if the application cache is working. We do this by doing:

```
AppCacheStatus status = (ApplicationCache) driver).getStatus();
```

3. The status should be equal to uncached when we load it.

4. The final class should look like the following:

```
import org.junit.*;
import org.openqa.selenium.*;

public class TestChapter10 {

  WebDriver driver;

  @Before
  public void setUp(){
    driver = new AndroidDriver();
    driver.get("http://book.theautomatedtester.co.uk/");
  }

  @After
  public void tearDown(){
    driver.quit();
  }

  @Test
  public void testAppCacheStatus(){
    AppCacheStatus status = (ApplicationCache)
      driver).getStatus();
    assertEqual(status AppCacheStatus.UNCACHED);
  }
}
```

What just happened?

We have just seen how we can get the application cache from the browser using the API built into the Selenium WebDriver. We will get an `enum` returned that relates to the current status that the browser returns. Now we know that we have the means to start to have a look at how our web application will act if it were to become offline.

Interacting with browser connections

Now that we can download and cache files using the application cache, it would be a good idea to see how well they work when there is no network connection. The mobile drivers have the ability to go into airplane mode. Hopefully, future versions of desktop browsers will have this ability too.

We will start by having a look at whether the browser is online.

Seeing if the browser is online

Seeing if a browser is online during a test can be quite useful when we are testing how our application works offline. This is useful for working against sites that may have the application cache configured and you want to check if the site works when offline. To know that, we first need to make sure we know how to check if the browser is currently online.

Let's see how this looks.

Time for action – seeing if the browser is online

In this section, we will have a look at seeing if the browser is online or offline. Currently, this only works on mobile drivers from Selenium WebDriver. In this section, we will need to cast the Selenium WebDriver object to `BrowserConnection` and then access the methods that are found on that object.

Let's get into action:

1. Create a new test class using the example code at the beginning of the chapter. We can call the class `TestBrowserConnection`.

2. Create a test method and add the following to it:

   ```
   assertTrue(((BrowserConnection) driver).isOnline());
   ```

3. Your class should look like the following and when you run the test method it will pass:

```
import org.junit.*;
import org.openqa.selenium.*;

public class TestChapter10 {

  WebDriver driver;

  @Before
  public void setUp(){
    driver = new AndroidDriver();
    driver.get("http://book.theautomatedtester.co.uk/");
  }

  @After
  public void tearDown(){
    driver.quit();
  }

  @Test
  public void testBrowserConnection(){
    assertTrue(((BrowserConnection) driver).isOnline());
  }
}
```

What just happened?

We have seen that by casting the `webdriver` object to `BrowserConnection`, we have access to a number of new methods. These methods allow us to see if the browser is currently online or offline. They also allow us to set the browser to online or offline, which will be the next section of this book.

Setting the browser offline or online

Now that we know how to see if the browser is online or offline, let us have a look at setting the browser connection to online or offline. This is not part of HTML5 technologies, but will allow us to use the previous online call, which is part of HTML 5, and to check if our application cache has downloaded the relevant files.

Let's see this in action.

Time for action – setting the browser connection to offline or online

In this section, we are going to turn the device's browser connectivity off. This means that we can check how the application works if it were offline. This is going to be a really useful feature as more and more applications try to take advantage of the move to mobile.

Let's see this in action.

1. We are going to create a new test method in the class that we created in the previous section.

2. In the test we are going to need to set the browser offline. We do this by casting to `BrowserConnection` and then using the method `setOnline()`. If we pass in `true`, it will set it online and if we set it to `false`, it will set the browser offline. Following is an example:

   ```
   ((BrowserConnection) driver).setOnline(false);
   ```

3. When you have finished, your class should look like the following:

   ```java
   import org.junit.*;
   import org.openqa.selenium.*;

   public class TestChapter10 {

     WebDriver driver;

     @Before
     public void setUp(){
       driver = new AndroidDriver();
       driver.get("http://book.theautomatedtester.co.uk/");
     }

     @After
     public void tearDown(){
       driver.quit();
     }

     @Test
     public void testBrowserConnectionOnline(){
       assertTrue(((BrowserConnection) driver).isOnline());
     }

     @Test
     Public void testTurnOffConnectivity(){
       BrowserConnection networkAwareDriver = (BrowserConnection)
         driver;
       networkAwareDriver.setOnline(false);
   ```

```
        assertFalse(networkAwareDriver.isOnline());
        networkAwareDriver.setOnline(true);
        assertFalse(networkAwareDriver.isOnline());


    }
}
```

What just happened?

We have seen that we can simply turn the browser connection on and off on these devices and check that the browser is in the correct state, either online or offline, before moving on with the test.

Now, we will move on to how to access some of the HTML5 storage technologies.

Working with WebStorage

Some of the other technologies that are being developed for HTML5 are related to WebStorage. There are three main WebStorage technologies:

◆ Local storage

◆ Session storage

◆ WebSQL

In this section of the chapter, we will only be working with the first two since WebSQL is not being implemented by all of the browser vendors. These technologies allow us to save to the users' hard disk and then retrieve what we stored.

Let's start using this.

Local storage

In this section, we are going to have a look at working through local storage to make sure that items we expect to be there are there. This is analogous to an integration test that accesses a database to check whether something has been sorted. `LocalStorage` allows data to be stored and the data is persisted between sessions and the browser being closed and reopened.

The Selenium WebDriver object called `LocalStorage` is used to access the local storage in the browser. The API is nearly a 1:1 match for the JavaScript API that comes with browsers.

Let's see this in action.

Time for action – accessing localStorage

Imagine that your application has stored something in the `localStorage` while the user has been interacting with the application. An example of this might be if you were working in a word processing application and it auto saves what you have typed to the box every so often. If your application were offline, it can still save the information.

Let's see how we would access this.

1. Create a new test class. You can use the example code at the beginning of the chapter to help you create it quicker.

2. Accessing the `LocalStorage` object will require us to case the `WebDriver` object to it. This is similar to what we saw with `BrowserConnection` previously.

    ```
    LocalStorage storageDriver = (LocalStorage) driver;
    storageDriver.size(); // returns 0 if there is nothing in there
    ```

3. Now run your test class. It should look something like the following:

    ```
    import org.junit.*;
    import org.openqa.selenium.*;

    public class TestChapter10 {

      WebDriver driver;

      @Before
      public void setUp(){
        driver = new AndroidDriver();
        driver.get("http://book.theautomatedtester.co.uk/
          localStorage.html");
      }

      @After
      public void tearDown(){
        driver.quit();
      }

      @Test
      public void testShouldReturnCurrentLocalStorageSize(){
        assertEqual(0, ((LocalStorage) driver).size());
      }
    }
    ```

What just happened?

We have just seen how we can access `LocalStorage`, the Selenium WebDriver API, for accessing the browsers' `localStorage` object. This means that we can have a look and check what the application has stored on the user's local storage. If were to log

Session storage

Session storage is a very similar technology to local storage. The main difference is that it does not persist. If you were to close the tab and then reopen it, while using Firefox for example, session storage items will not be available where local storage will still be available.

Let's see how we can work with it.

Time for action – accessing sessionStorage

Imagine again that you are working against a word processing application but instead of it auto saving the text that you type to somewhere that is persisted, you only save it briefly waiting for the user to click save.

Let us see how we can use it.

1. Let's just add a new `testMethod` to the class we created in the previous section. We can call it `testShouldAccessSessionStorage()`.

2. We will need to cast the `WebDriver` object to a `SessionStorage` object, so we can start accessing the methods it has available like the following:

    ```
    SessionStorage storage = (SessionStorage) driver;
    assertEquals(0, storage.size());
    ```

3. Let's create our test and run it. It should look like the following:

    ```
    import org.junit.*;
    import org.openqa.selenium.*;


    public class TestChapter10 {

      WebDriver driver;

      @Before
      public void setUp(){
        driver = new AndroidDriver();
        driver.get("http://book.theautomatedtester.co.uk/
          localStorage.html");
    ```

```
    }

    @After
    public void tearDown(){
      driver.quit();
    }

    @Test
    public void testShouldReturnCurrentLocalStorageSize(){
      assertEqual(0, ((SessionStorage) driver).size());
    }
  }
```

What just happened?

We have just seen that the `SessionStorage` object acts a lot like the `localStorage` object that we worked with in the previous section of the chapter. We were able to get the `SessionStorage` methods by casting the Selenium `WebDriver` object. This gives us access to methods that map over to the JavaScript API available in the browser.

Summary

We learnt a lot in this chapter about using the HTML5 API that comes with Selenium WebDriver. These are helper methods that make our lives significantly easier when working against application cache or against web storage mechanisms.

Specifically, we covered:

♦ **Application cache API**: We had a look at how we can access the browsers' application cache to see if it is downloading items into the cache or if the current app is uncached.

♦ **Browser connections**: Web applications, with the help of HTML5 technologies, are getting the ability to work when they are offline. We have seen how, with the help of application cache, we can load pages from the cache. We can also see if the browser is currently online or offline, and on the mobile devices be able to turn them to airplane mode.

♦ **WebStorage**: In this section we had a look at how we can access the `WebStorage` object that has been added to the HTML5 specification. Specifically, we had a look at `localStorage` and `sessionStorage`. Selenium WebDriver has tried to emulate the APIs available in the browser in the Selenium WebDriver APIs.

If you want to read more on session storage I recommend reading `https://developer.mozilla.org/en-US/docs/DOM/` `Storage#sessionStorage`.

Now that we've learnt about working with HTML5, we're ready to work through the final advanced topics—which is the topic of the next chapter.

11
Advanced Topics

In this chapter we are going to have a look at a number of advanced topics that we can do with Selenium WebDriver. These topics are not required in order to use Selenium WebDriver, but will be useful when there are problems with testing your application and you need to get some more information.

In this chapter, we shall learn:

- ◆ Capturing screenshots
- ◆ Using XVFB with Selenium
- ◆ Working with Browsermob Proxy

So let's get on with it...

Important preliminary points

Before we start it will be good to download all the necessary items. Please download the latest from Browsermob Proxy: `https://github.com/webmetrics/browsermob-proxy/downloads`.

XVFB—sudo apt-get install xvfb. XVFB only really works reliably on Linux. You could potentially get this to work on OS X but it does not, as of writing this chapter, have great support. This will not work on Windows unfortunately.

```
davidburns@ubuntu:~$ sudo apt-get install xvfb
Reading package lists... Done
Building dependency tree
Reading state information... Done
The following NEW packages will be installed:
  xvfb
0 upgraded, 1 newly installed, 0 to remove and 0 not upgraded.
Need to get 866 kB of archives.
After this operation, 2,068 kB of additional disk space will be used.
Get:1 http://us.archive.ubuntu.com/ubuntu/ oneiric-updates/main xvfb amd64 2:1.10.4-1ubuntu4.2 [866 kB]
Fetched 866 kB in 3s (230 kB/s)
Selecting previously deselected package xvfb.
(Reading database ... 228914 files and directories currently installed.)
Unpacking xvfb (from .../xvfb_2%3a1.10.4-1ubuntu4.2_amd64.deb) ...
Processing triggers for man-db ...
Setting up xvfb (2:1.10.4-1ubuntu4.2) ...
davidburns@ubuntu:~$
```

Capturing screenshots

A lot of the time our Selenium remote control browsers will be running on different machines than the machine that starts the tests. This is because you, as a developer or tester, need a mechanism to have a screenshot of what the error looks like when the test failed. Images that are captured are saved in PNG format.

Unfortunately capturing screenshots in Selenium is limited to real browsers such as Mozilla Firefox, Google Chrome, and Internet Explorer. This is because these browsers have libraries that Selenium can use to take screenshots. As more libraries are added to Selenium for different browsers, you will be able to take more screenshots. They will use the same API call so there will be no need to change your tests.

Screenshots capability lives within an interface called TakesScreenshot. We will cast the driver to this and then use the interface to access getScreenshotAs() method. You will also need to import the following library:

```
import static openqa.selenium.OutputType.*;
```

Capturing base64 version of images

In this section we are going to have a look at capturing a base64 representation of an image. Base64 is a group of encoding schemes that allow us to represent binary data as ASCII. A common use for them in web applications is to place data URLs as the source for images to save on downloads that the browser has to do when it is parsing the HTML.

Time for action – capturing images as base64 strings

Imagine that you want to take a screenshot on Selenium Grid. When you take the screenshot, you will not want it to be saved to the hard drive of the Selenium Grid node. You will want it to be moved back to where your tests are, especially if you are using it with a Continuous Integration Box.

1. Open up Intellij and create a new Java test class.

2. We will now add a new line for taking a screenshot:

    ```
    driver.get(http://book.theautomatedtester.co.uk);
    String screenshotBase64 = ((Screenshot)
       driver).getScreenshotAs(base64);
    ```

3. If you set a breakpoint on the previous line, you will be able to see what the string looks like.

What just happened?

We have just managed to take a screenshot and have it returned as a base64 string. This will allow us to take a screenshot on a remote machine and then transport the resultant image back to where the test is being run from.

Saving the screenshot to bytes

Now that we have had a look at capturing screenshots to base64 strings, let's have a look at capturing them as bytes. Having them as bytes means that we can transform them into a number of different things as we see fit.

Time for action – saving images to bytes

Imagine that you want to do some in-depth analysis of the UI by taking screenshots. This is something that has been done a number of times in different projects. For example, you take a screenshot, then make changes, and then take more screenshots along the way.

1. Open up Intellij and create a new Java test class.

2. We will now add a new line for taking a screenshot:

    ```
    driver.get(http://book.theautomatedtester.co.uk);
    Bytes screenbytes = ((Screenshot)driver).getScreenshotAs(bytes);
    ```

3. If you set a breakpoint on the previous line, you will be able to see what the string looks like.

What just happened?

Now that we have seen what it takes to take a screenshot of the page from the browser, we have managed to take a screenshot and then push the result into a `bytes` variable. We can then perform histogram type checks against the bytes and anything else that we want.

We can also push the bytes into a stream to save it to file or we can have a look at taking screenshots straight to files.

Saving screenshots to files

Saving screenshots to file is probably the most common way to save a file. This approach will save the file to disk straight away. When we save the screenshot as a file, we are returned a `file` object.

We can then use it straight away to do anything like `getPath()` or do what we need.

Time for action – saving a screenshot to file

In this section we will have a look at how we can go about saving a file to disk. This is the most common thing that people do when saving screenshots. One thing to note is that if you are using RemoteWebDriver, this will save the file on the same machine as the Selenium Server.

1. Open up Intellij and create a new Java test class.
2. We will now add a new line for taking a screenshot:

```
driver.get(http://book.theautomatedtester.co.uk);
File savedImage = ((Screenshot)driver).getScreenshotAs(file);
```

3. If you set a breakpoint on the previous line, you will be able to see what the string looks like.

What just happened?

We have just seen what is probably going to be the most common way to save screenshots when we take them. When we take the screenshot, the image is saved to disk and we are returned the `file` object that has access to that image.

If you would like to move the file when it is created, you can use the following code snippet:

```
File imageFile = ((TakesScreenshot) driver)
   .getScreenshotAs(OutputType.FILE);
String failureImageFileName = "testfailureimage.png";

File failureImageFile = new File(failureImageFileName);
FileUtils.moveFile(imageFile, failureImageFile);
```

Pop quiz – saving screenshots

1. What is the easiest approach to saving images?

    a. Base64 String

    b. Bytes

    c. File

2. If you want to move a screenshot over Selenium grid, which is the best output type to choose?

Using XVFB with Selenium

The following section of this book requires that we do this work in Linux as the requirements are only available on that platform. When Selenium is running on your machine, you will see that it always runs on your screen. If you want to push the running of your tests to a background, then you will need to use something like XVFB. **XVFB** stands for **X11 Virtual Frame Buffer**.

This allows us to run tests with a real browser without it trying to steal focus from you. FirefoxDriver, for example, forces the browser to the foreground to help the native events.

Time for action – setting up XVFB server

We will have to make sure that we have XVFB running on our machine. This should be fairly trivial to getting it right.

1. Open a terminal.

2. In the terminal, we will run the following command:

    ```
    Xvfb :1 -screen 0 1600x1200x32
    ```

3. The server will listen for connections as server number 1, and screen 0 will be depth 32 1600x1200.

4. You should see something like this in your terminal:

```
davidburns@ubuntu:~$ Xvfb :2 -screen 1 1600x1200x16
[dix] Could not init font path element /usr/share/fonts/X11/cyrillic, removing f
rom list!
[dix] Could not init font path element /usr/share/fonts/X11/100dpi/:unscaled, re
moving from list!
[dix] Could not init font path element /usr/share/fonts/X11/75dpi/:unscaled, rem
oving from list!
[dix] Could not init font path element /usr/share/fonts/X11/100dpi, removing fro
m list!
[dix] Could not init font path element /usr/share/fonts/X11/75dpi, removing from
 list!
```

What just happened?

We have just seen what it takes to setup XVFB running on our machines. We have just told it to start an XVFB server and set up a screen on that server. If you want to set up XVFB in different ways, I recommend reading the manual at http://www.xfree86.org/4.0.1/Xvfb.1.html.

Running tests in XVFB

Now that we have the server up and running, we can have a look at making sure that when we run our tests they use the new display.

Time for action – running tests with XVFB

We will have to make sure that we have XVFB running on the machine.

1. Open a terminal.

2. We need to export the display so that everything that is launched from it uses the one that we have set up earlier. We do this with:

   `Export DISPLAY=0.1`

3. Now we just need to run our tests. You will see that the browser may launch in the dock but it should not actually be visible.

What just happened?

We have successfully managed to get our tests running using XVFB. We saw that the tests that we were running, and launching a browser on our displays, still finished with the same results as before.

This can be useful for situations where you may have your tests running on change and you know that the browser will not try stealing focus.

Pop quiz – using XVFB

1. What does XVFB stand for?
2. What argument do we need to pass in when starting the XVFB to have it startup on a specific display?

Have a go hero – running tests in parallel with XVFB

Now that we know how to run tests with XVFB, try getting this running while running tests in parallel and see how it works together!

Working with BrowserMob Proxy

Patrick Lightbody, one of the core originators of Selenium and creator of Selenium RC with Paul Hammant, created the BrowserMob proxy while working on his startup BrowserMob. BrowserMob Proxy allows you to control the way that traffic is filtered to the browser.

We can also change the headers that are supplied to the server. This allows us to do a large number of things.

Creating a proxy

When working with BrowserMob Proxy we will need to make sure that we start the proxy so that we can use the API and change what we need.

Time for action – starting the proxy

We are going to need to start the proxy and make sure that we can then interact with it.

1. Create a new Project in Intellij.
2. Add the BrowserMob JARs to the project so that we can use it:

   ```
   ProxyServer proxy = New ProxyServer(9876);
   proxy.start();
   ```

3. When we want to stop the server we just call:

   ```
   proxy.stop()
   ```

What just happened?

We have successfully started the server by passing in the port. The server needs to be started before we can do any of the different tasks that we will be doing in future sections of the book.

Capturing network traffic

One of the most useful things in Selenium Remote Control is the ability to capture the network traffic of the application that you are testing. It was removed since it is not required to do browser automation, but it was nice to have.

To capture network traffic, we need to proxy all traffic through BrowserMob Proxy. The way that BrowserMob Proxy does this is by capturing the network traffic and pushing it into a format called **HTTP Archive**, or most commonly known as **HAR**. A HAR file is JSON format that is the standard way to represent network traffic.

HAR captures lot of information that can be used for different purposes, so we will learn how to capture it next.

Time for action – capturing network traffic

Imagine that you wanted to see if there was anything on the page that was not found. This could be images, CSS files, or JavaScript files. These things are not visible when working with a page, and it can be interesting with unexpected bugs. We will now see how we can create a HAR file and then capture it.

Since the HAR will return the JSON we need, we just need to parse the JSON returned to get what we want.

1. Using the project we created previously, we are going to add a few more lines to get what we want.

2. We need tell Selenium WebDriver that we have a proxy that it has to use. We do that with:

   ```
   FirefoxProfile profile = new FirefoxProfile();
   profile.setProxy(proxy.seleniumProxy);
   ```

3. We need to tell the proxy to create a new HAR file for us. We do this by adding the following line:

   ```
   Proxy.newHar("PageName"); // PageName is the name of the page we
                             //want to capture
   ```

4. We then need to load a page, we can do this by clicking on a link calling `get()`.

5. Now we need to call `proxy.getHar()`. This will return the HAR that we wanted.

6. Your code should look like this:

```
FirefoxProfile profile = new FirefoxProfile();
profile.setProxy(proxy.seleniumProxy);
WebDriver driver = new FirefoxDriver(profile);
proxy.newHar("PageName");
driver.get("http://book.theautomatedtester.co.uk
    proxy.getHar();
```

7. And your HAR, once put through a JSON Viewer should look like this:

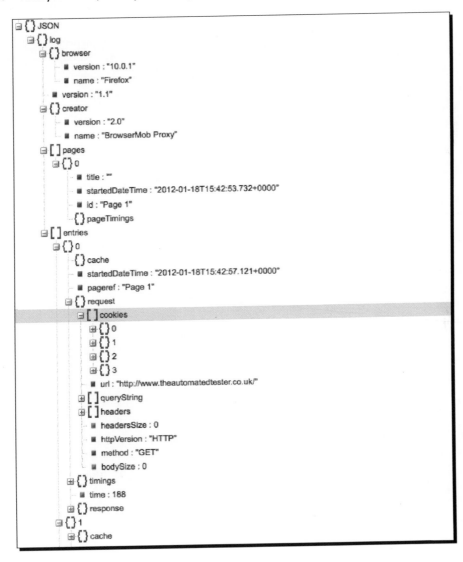

What just happened?

We have just managed to capture the network traffic while we are running our tests. This can be really useful if you want to see if there are any 404 responses when we are loading our application under test. This can be useful if you are moving things about or if you are doing a smoke test after you have deployed your application to production.

Pop quiz – capturing Network Traffic

1. What is the name of the JSON format for showing network traffic?
2. What is the call that tells BrowserMob Proxy to start recording the traffic?

Have a go hero – doing more with BrowserMob Proxy

Now that we have managed to get the proxy started and managed to record the network traffic that is going through to the browser, let us have a look at getting the proxy to slow down the time that a response takes to get through. BrowserMob Proxy supports this and Intellij will be able to help with what parts of the API to use.

Summary

We learnt a lot in this chapter about some of the advanced topics that we may need in tougher times!

Specifically, we covered:

- **Saving screenshots**: We have learnt how to save screenshots of our web applications programmatically. This allows us to know when something happens and we need to see what could be the reason!

- **Using XVFB**: In this section, we learnt how to use XVFB to have a virtual display to run our tests in. This can be really useful if you want to be able to run Selenium WebDriver and not worry that when the tests run the browser might suddenly steal focus. This is useful if you are running a number of tests on a single machine and they need to use native events that Selenium WebDriver tries to do on Windows and Linux.

- **BrowserMob Proxy**: In this section, we had a look at how we can replicate Selenium Remote Control's `captureNetworkTraffic()` method that will allow us to see what the browser downloaded during a page load. This is useful if you are doing web performance analysis during tests.

We should also note that BrowserMob Proxy can do a lot more than record network traffic. It can block content from certain URLs, like ad networks, which can improve the speed at which tests run. This might be something to consider if your tests take hours and it is tracked down to a web performance issue.

Now that we've learnt about these topics, you should feel extremely confident in using Selenium WebDriver and can test it against a number of the different web applications out there!

A

Migrating from Remote Control to WebDriver

Selenium Remote Control has been around for a number of years. This means that there is a large amount of tests out there written for the API. If you ever have to migrate your test suite, then the following chapter will give you the insight that you need.

In this chapter, we shall cover WebDriver Backed Selenium.

Before we work through this chapter, it might be a good idea to go through *Chapter 4, Design Patterns* again as this will minimize the amount of work that is required as we move to WebDriver. So let's get on with it...

WebDriverBackedSelenium

Unfortunately, we have spent a considerable time in the past few years developing Selenium Remote Control tests, and converting them over to the new style of Selenium WebDriver may not be feasible. The WebDriver API is fundamentally different in its design compared to Selenium RC.

With this in mind, the Selenium Core development team has created the `WebDriverBackedSelenium` object that we can use. This allows us to create our tests with Selenium Remote Control syntax that we know but have some of the benefits of WebDriver with a very minor change to what you currently have.

```
String baseUrl = "http://book.theautomatedtester.co.uk";
String remoteControl = "localhost";
Int port = 4444;
String browser = "*firefox";
Selenium selenium = new DefaultSelenium(remoteControl, port ,
   browser ,baseUrl);
selenium.start();
selenium.open("/");
selenium.click("link=chapter1");
// rest of the test code
```

We then need to change our tests to the following:

```
WebDriver driver = new FirefoxDriver();
String baseUrl = "http://book.theautomatedtester.co.uk";
Selenium selenium = new WebDriverBackedSelenium(driver,baseUrl);
selenium.open("/");
selenium.click("link=chapter1");
// rest of the test code
```

Let's try to convert one of our Selenium Remote Control tests.

Time for action – converting tests to Selenium WebDriver using WebDriverBackedSelenium

Let's take one of our Selenium Remote Control tests and change it to use `WebDriverBackedSelenium`. This should be a simple change:

```
import com.thoughtworks.selenium.*;
import org.junit.*;

public class TestSeleniumWebDriver {
   // We can name this file what we want

   Selenium selenium;

   @Before
   public void setup(){
      selenium = new DefaultSelenium("localhost",4444,"*chrome",
         "http://book.theautomatedtester.co.uk");
```

```
    selenium.start();
  }

  @Test
  public void shouldOpenChapter2LinkAndVerifyAButton(){
    /* This will contain some actions for us. We are going
     * to be concentrating on the @Before and @After methods
  }

  @After
  public void teardown(){
    selenium.stop();
  }
}
```

1. Open IDEA and load your example.

2. Create a new external library for the Selenium binaries. We learnt how to do this in *Chapter 3, Overview of Selenium WebDriver*.

3. Add the variable WebDriver driver at the top of your class.

4. Change your `setup()` to look like the following:

```
@Before
public void setup(){
  driver = new FirefoxDriver();
  selenium = new WebDriverBackedSelenium(driver,
    http://book.theautomatedtester.co.uk)
}
```

5. Change the `teardown()` to:

```
@After
public void teardown(){
  driver.quit();
}
```

6. Run your tests.

What just happened?

We have seen how with very little change to our tests we have got our old Selenium Remote Control tests working using the new Selenium WebDriver drivers. The `WebDriverBackedSelenium` object has a mapping of the Selenium Remote Control API to the Selenium WebDriver API.

When the browser starts you will see the WebDriver extension in the bottom right of the browser. When it is processing commands, it will turn red and when it isn't it will be black. It should look like the following screenshot:

There are a few items that are not fully supported by `WebDriverBackedSelenium`, but hopefully as more and more work is done to the framework these will be less noticeable. This is available to all languages that can communicate with the remote server.

Pop quiz – how do you use WebDriverBackedSelenium

1. How do you use the `WebDriverBackedSelenium`?

Summary

We have seen that we can easily move from tests that we created in the past using the Selenium Remote Control API.

Specifically, we covered:

◆   **Switching to WebDriverBackedSelenium**: In this section, we saw that with only a few lines changed within our tests we can suddenly be running with Selenium WebDriver, the new API in the Selenium project. This will not allow us to fully migrate our tests but gives us a starting point. Remember that `WebDriverBackedSelenium` can work in all languages. You can either use the object or inject a WebDriver Object into the Selenium Object and have the Selenium Server do all of the work for you.

B
Pop Quiz Answers

Chapter 1

Pop quiz – Selenium IDE

1. **Answer:** c

Pop quiz – verifying and asserting

1. **Answer:** b
2. **Answer:** Verify allows a test to continue and keep track of all verify errors. Assert will stop a test immediately when the assert fails.
3. **Answer:** b

Pop quiz – waiting for elements

1. **Answer:** a

Pop quiz – Test Suites

1. **Answer:** Click on the button with the arrow and three solid green lines.

Chapter 2

Pop quiz – using the Find button

1. **Answer:** d

Pop quiz – finding Elements with DOM JavaScript

1. **Answer:** c

Pop quiz – using XPath Axis

1. **Answer:** a and b

Pop quiz – using locators

1. **Answer:** a
2. **Answer:** `//input/following-sibling::input`
3. **Answer:** `css=input + input`

Chapter 3

Pop quiz – setting up the test project

1. **Answer:** In the `test` folder.

Chapter 4

Pop quiz – Page Object design pattern

1. **Answer:** The Page Object design pattern gives us a way to abstract our tests away so that we can make these tests more maintainable. We can make tests that only require updating if new steps have been added, otherwise it just requires the page object to be updated.

Pop quiz – Page Factories

1. **Answer:** `@FindBy(how=How.ID, using='myId')`

2. **Answer:** `@CacheLookup`

3. **Answer:** `PageFactory.initElements();`

Chapter 5

Pop quiz – finding elements using helper methods

1. **Answer:** b

2. **Answer:** c

3. **Answer:** No, it will not throw an exception. It will return an empty list.

Chapter 6

Pop quiz – working with FirefoxDriver

1. **Answer:** Create a profile object and call `setPreference()` method with the details needed.

2. **Answer:** We can use the `FirefoxBinary` class to tell it where to look.

Pop quiz – using ChromeDriver

1. **Answer:** ChromeOptions

2. **Answer:** The `PATH` environment variable needs to be set with where the ChromeDriver executable lives. This is so that when we call ChromeDriver with our Java code, it will load the relevant executable and load the browser as quickly as possible.

Pop quiz – working with OperaDriver

1. **Answer:** Use the latest stable version of Opera.

2. **Answer:** Use the `OperaProfile` object and update the preferences where needed.

Pop quiz – working with InternetExplorerDriver

3. **Answer:** All versions of IE6, IE7, IE8, and IE9 for both 32-bit and 64-bit installations.

Chapter 7

Pop quiz – working with Android

1. **Answer:** `./android create avd -n my_android -t 14 -c 100M`

2. **Answer:** a

3. **Answer:** c

4. **Answer:**

   ```
   adb -s <serialId> shell am start -a android.intent.action.MAIN
   -n org.openqa.selenium.android.app/.MainActivity
   ```

5. **Answer:** c

Chapter 8

Pop quiz – using Selenium Grid 2

1. **Answer:** `java –jar selenium-server.jar -role hub`

2. **Answer:** `http://nameofmachine:4444/grid/console` where `nameofmachine` is the name of the machine that is running the hub. If it is on the same machine as you are currently on put localhost or 127.0.0.1.

3. **Answer:** `port 4444`

4. **Answer:** `-browser browserName="internet explorer", maxInstances=1,platform=WINDOWS`

Chapter 9

Pop quiz – using Action Chains

1. **Answer:** Action

2. **Answer:** `build()`

3. **Answer:** `Perform()3`

4. **Answer.** `moveByOffset()`

Chapter 11

Pop quiz – saving screenshots

1. **Answer:** c
2. **Answer:** Base64

Pop quiz – using XVFB

1. **Answer:** X11 Virtual Frame Buffer
2. **Answer:** -screen

Pop quiz – capturing Network Traffic

1. **Answer:** HTTP Archive or HAR
2. **Answer:** newHar()

Appendix A

Pop quiz – how do you use WebDriverBackedSelenium

1. **Answer:** Create a new instance of the browser you want to use using Selenium WebDriver. Then pass this into the WebDriverBackedSelenium with the URL that you would like to test. It will look like this:

```
@Before
    public void setup(){
      driver = new FirefoxDriver();
      selenium = new WebDriverBackedSelenium(driver,
        http://book.theautomatedtester.co.uk)
    }
```

Index

XPath
  about 97
  used, for nth element type finding 47, 48
XPath Axis
  using, for element search 50
XPath queries
  Axis list 51
  element attributes, using 48
XVFB
  about 182
  using, with Selenium 185

XVFB using, with Selenium
  about 185
  tests, running in XVFB 186
  XVFB server, setting up 185, 186

Y

YAML file
  Selenium Grid 2, using 152

Thank you for buying
Selenium 2 Testing Tools Beginner's Guide

About Packt Publishing

Packt, pronounced 'packed', published its first book "*Mastering phpMyAdmin for Effective MySQL Management*" in April 2004 and subsequently continued to specialize in publishing highly focused books on specific technologies and solutions.

Our books and publications share the experiences of your fellow IT professionals in adapting and customizing today's systems, applications, and frameworks. Our solution based books give you the knowledge and power to customize the software and technologies you're using to get the job done. Packt books are more specific and less general than the IT books you have seen in the past. Our unique business model allows us to bring you more focused information, giving you more of what you need to know, and less of what you don't.

Packt is a modern, yet unique publishing company, which focuses on producing quality, cutting-edge books for communities of developers, administrators, and newbies alike. For more information, please visit our website: www.packtpub.com.

About Packt Open Source

In 2010, Packt launched two new brands, Packt Open Source and Packt Enterprise, in order to continue its focus on specialization. This book is part of the Packt Open Source brand, home to books published on software built around Open Source licences, and offering information to anybody from advanced developers to budding web designers. The Open Source brand also runs Packt's Open Source Royalty Scheme, by which Packt gives a royalty to each Open Source project about whose software a book is sold.

Writing for Packt

We welcome all inquiries from people who are interested in authoring. Book proposals should be sent to author@packtpub.com. If your book idea is still at an early stage and you would like to discuss it first before writing a formal book proposal, contact us; one of our commissioning editors will get in touch with you.

We're not just looking for published authors; if you have strong technical skills but no writing experience, our experienced editors can help you develop a writing career, or simply get some additional reward for your expertise.

Selenium 1.0 Testing Tools: Beginner's Guide

ISBN: 978-1-84951-026-4   Paperback: 232 pages

Take your web applications with multiple browsers using the Selenium Framework to ensure the quality of web applications

1. Save your valuable time by using Selenium to record, tweak and replay your test scripts

2. Get rid of any bugs deteriorating the quality of your web applications

3. Take your web applications one step closer to perfection using Selenium tests

4. Packed with detailed working examples that illustrate the techniques and tools for debugging

Python Testing Cookbook

ISBN: 978-1-84951-466-8   Paperback: 346 pages

Over 70 simple but incredibly effective recipes for taking control of automated testing using powerful Python testing tools

1. Learn to write tests at every level using a variety of Python testing tools

2. The first book to include detailed screenshots and recipes for using Jenkins continuous integration server (formerly known as Hudson)

3. Explore innovative ways to introduce automated testing to legacy systems

4. Written by Greg L. Turnquist – senior software engineer and author of Spring Python 1.1

Please check **www.PacktPub.com** for information on our titles

Agile Web Application Development with Yii1.1 and PHP5

ISBN: 978-1-84719-958-4   Paperback: 368 pages

Fast-track your web application development by harnessing the power of the Yii PHP Framework

1. A step-by-step guide to creating a modern, sophisticated web application using an incremental and iterative approach to software development

2. Build a real-world, user-based, database-driven project task management application using the Yii development framework

3. Take a test-driven design (TDD) approach to software development utilizing the Yii testing framework

Yii 1.1 Application Development Cookbook

ISBN: 978-1-84951-548-1   Paperback: 392 pages

Over 80 recipes to help you master using the Yii PHP framework

1. Learn to use Yii more efficiently through plentiful Yii recipes on diverse topics

2. Make the most efficient use of your controller and views and reuse them

3. Automate error tracking and understand the Yii log and stack trace

4. Full of practically useful solutions and concepts that you can use in your application, with clearly explained code and all the necessary screenshots

Please check **www.PacktPub.com** for information on our titles

Printed in Great Britain
by Amazon.co.uk, Ltd.,
Marston Gate.